Mental Fascination

Mental Fascination

BY

WILLIAM WALKER ATKINSON

GYAN

Published by

GYAN

Gyan Publishing House
5, Ansari Road
Daryaganj, New Delhi-110002
Phone: 011-47034999, 9811692060
E-mail: books@gyanbooks.com

Distribution Network
gyanbooks.com
India, USA, Canada, UK, Australia

ISBN: 978-93-6208-512-2 (HB)
First Published, 1907

2nd Impression 2024

Printed at: Gyan Press, Delhi.

MENTAL FASCINATION
Author: WILLIAM WALKER ATKINSON

MENTAL FASCINATION

BY

WILLIAM WALKER ATKINSON

AUTHOR OF

"THE SECRET OF MENTAL MAGIC,"
ETC., ETC.

Being the First Manual in the nature of a Supplement or Sequel to
"THE SECRET OF MENTAL MAGIC,"
and designed as
SPECIAL INSTRUCTION
for the students of that work

WILLIAM WALKER ATKINSON
MASONIC TEMPLE
CHICAGO, ILL.
1907

CONTENTS.

PREFACE.

This book is *"Side-Light Manual No. 1,"* accompanying my main work entitled "THE SECRET OF MENTAL MAGIC," and being in the nature of a sequel, supplement, or "side-light" thereto. The *"Side-Light Manuals"* of which this is the first, are designed to bring out the details, and special features of several of the "lessons" of which "THE SECRET OF MENTAL MAGIC" is composed; and to give something in the nature of Special Instruction regarding the actual operation or workings of the principles referred to in the lessons of my main work. The present manual bears the above mentioned relation to that lesson in my main work entitled "Personal Influence."

In order to obviate the repetition of the information contained in my main work, I have been obliged to constantly refer to the latter. This would be inexcusable were the present book offered as a separate and independent work, for it might be justly considered as an effort to force my main work upon the attention of the reader, for the purpose of increasing its sale. But, inasmuch as the present book is advertised as a *"Side-Light,"* and its relation to my main work is plainly stated in every notice—and particularly as its sale will be almost exclusively among *those who have already purchased and studied my main work*—I think I may reasonably ask to be absolved from such suspicion.

I think that I have condensed much valuable information within the pages of this book, and I trust that my readers will like the work as well as do I. But, be that as it may, I defy anyone to read it without gaining a strong, practical realization of the powerful part, for good or ill, that Mental Fascination is playing in this Twentieth Century world of ours. And I feel that the majority will agree with me that it is time that this potent influence should be studied, understood, mastered and its "sting" extracted by such an universal knowledge of its principles as will serve to destroy its improper employment. To those who may consider this rather "dangerous knowledge" to be spread broadcast, I will say that Ignorance is no protection—I believe that in all cases the best way to dispel Darkness, and all that goes with it, is to Turn on the Light.

And this, then, is the Spirit in which this book has been written. May you so receive it.

William Walker Atkinson.

Chicago, Ill., U. S. A., May 13, 1907.

MENTAL FASCINATION

CHAPTER I.

WHAT IS "MENTAL FASCINATION?"

"Fascination" means "the act of Fascinating, or state of being Fascinated." The word "Fascinate" springs from the Latin word *"Fascinare,"* meaning "to enchant; bewitch, charm by eyes or tongue; captivate, attract," etc. The definition of the English word, "Fascinate," is as follows: "To act upon by some powerful or irresistible influence; to influence by an irresistible charm; to allure, or excite, irresistibly or powerfully; to charm, captivate, or attract, powerfully; to influence the imagination, reason or will of another, in an uncontrollable manner; to enchant, captivate or allure, powerfully or irresistibly."

The above definition is condensed from a number of the best dictionaries, and gives the cream of the idea embodied in the word.

MY DEFINITION.

In this manual I shall use the term "Mental Fascination" is the sense of: *The action of a Mental*

Force that powerfully influences the imagination, desire, or will of another. This is my own broad definition which includes all the varied phenomena of Personal Magnetism, Psychological Influence, Hypnotism, Mesmerism, Charming, etc., etc., all of which I hold to be but varying phases of phenomena of one Force. These things are all a "bit off the same piece," in spite of the claims to the contrary on the part of those who did not like the relationship.

THE NATURE OF THE FORCE.

What is the nature of the Force which produces that which we call Mental Fascination, which latter I have defined as "The action of a Mental Force that powerfully influences the imagination, desire or will of another?" Mental Fascination is the manifestation —what is the nature of the Mental Force that powerfully influences?

As you will see in some of the following chapters, there have been many theories advanced to account for this Force, the theories varying from "magnetic fluids" to mere simple suggestions on the part of the influencing person. Nearly every writer on the subject has had his own pet theory. But although these theories varied and differed greatly, the effects produced were about the same, which naturally leads us to look for some common basic principle operating under all the forms, regardless of the many theories advanced by those producing the effects. It is the old story here, as elsewhere.

A man finds that he is able to produce certain phenomena, by certain methods. He works along practical lines for a time, endeavoring to perfect his methods and increase the variety and effectiveness of the phenomena. When he has advanced along these lines, he begins to look around him for a theory to fit the facts of the case, and here is where he usually makes his mistake. He evolves some fantastic theory, which seems to him to account for the effects produced, and then he endeavors to fit the facts into the theory. If the facts will not so fit in, well, so much the worse for the facts—and he either discards the non-conforming facts, or else ignores or denies them. This has been the course of theorists since the beginning. After a while, some man of a more scientific mind examines the recorded facts, and discovers the true underlying principle, and reconciles the differing theories of the original theorists by a new synthesis which combines the true principles in all the other theories, discarding the pet hobbies or prejudices of the previous authorities. And so it is in the case of Mental Fascination, as we shall see.

THE UNDERLYING THEORY.

I shall not have much to say about theory in this book. I have explained the theory and principle underlying Mental Fascination, in my larger book entitled "The Secret of Mental Magic," of which this little manual is a "Side Light." In that book I have explained that the Underlying Force beneath all forms of Mental Magic—and Mental Fascination is one of those forms—is the Universal Mentative Energy, of which, and in which, each Individual Mind is a Center of Activity. I have also explained that the Mentative Energy of each Individual Mind is, and may be, transmitted from one person to another by means of Mentative Currents, or Waves. And that these Mentative Currents and Waves tend to "induce" in the minds of other persons, the emotions or feelings existing in the Mental States of the person sending out the waves or currents.

THE MENTAL POLES.

I have also explained that there are two Mental Poles known as the Motive and Emotive Poles, respectively, which manifest Will-Power and Desire Force, respectively. Desire Force acts in the direction of drawing, pulling, attracting, luring, coaxing, charming, etc.; while Will Power acts in the direction of compelling, forcing, driving, impelling, commanding, demanding, etc. Desire always *draws its object toward itself;* while Will always *overpowers and compels its object,* generally in the sense of driving it into action. In Mental Fascination both Desire Force, and Will Power are employed—generally in combination. Desire Force has been called the Feminine phase of Mentative Energy; and Will Power the Masculine. And in this as in everything else, the combination of the two qualities produces the most marked results. The student will be able to distinguish between the action of these two phases of the force, as he reads the pages of this book, in which instances of Mental Fascination are given.

This is all that I shall have to say about theory in this book, except where the various points are brought out in illustrating the examples given. I must refer my students to my "Secret of Mental Magic" for details of theory and principle. The present book deals with the "HOW?" rather than the "Why?"

CHAPTER II.

MENTAL FASCINATION AMONG THE ANIMALS.

Even before the human race was evolved, Mental Fascination was known instinctively to the lower forms of life. It is said that the cells in the blood of living things become aware of the presence of each other, at distances which must preclude any theory of ordinary sense "awareness." Not only do they recognize or "sense" the presence of each other, but they seem to be attracted toward each other by some force, or fascination, which must operate along the lines of Desire and Will. Eminent scientists inform us that even the atoms manifest an attraction for each other, varying in degree according to the nature of the respective atoms. And the same authorities tell us that this attracting operates along the lines of a "desire" for each other, and a "will" which causes them to fly to each other. Is it not reasonable to suppose that in this instinctive manifestation of Attraction, and the response to Attraction, among the Atoms there is to be found the elemental principle of Mental Fascination, and Magnetic Attraction, related to the human tion? And are not the phenomena of Electrical Attrac- phenomena by a long series of links in a grand chain?

THE TWO PHASES.

But, leaving the above questions without further consideration, we may find an abundance of proof among the higher forms of the "lower animals." Among the animals we find many instances of the power of "charming" or "fascinating," both of which I hold to be but varying forms of manifestation of Mental Fascination as I use the term, *i. e.,* "The action of a Mental Force that powerfully influences the imagination, desire, or will of another." This Mental Fascination, among the animals, manifests along two lines, *viz.,* (1) along the lines of Desire operating in the direction of Sex manifestation, such as the winning of mates, etc.; and (2) along the lines of Will operation in the direction of overcoming the Prey of the animal, such as the "charming" of birds by serpents, or of smaller animals by tigers, etc. These cases are capable of liberal illustration and proof, and natural history affords us full authority for accepting the same.

INSTANCES OF ANIMAL FASCINATION.

I recently read an account of a naturalist, who related that one day in a tropical country he noticed a winged insect circling around and around a scorpion.

After a bit, the insect made a series of desperate plunges at the scorpion, as if in a frantic desire to terminate the charm; the scorpion soon striking down the insect, and afterwards devouring it. It is related by travelers that when one comes suddenly in the presence of a lion, tiger, or leopard, his legs seem paralyzed, and the eyes of the beast seem to exert a peculiar fascination and power over him. I have seen a mouse manifest the same emotion in the presence of a cat; and the same is true of a rat in the presence of a ferret, or similar enemy. On the other hand, every observer has noticed the wonderful "charming" power that animals exert over others of their kind, of the opposite sex. If you have ever witnessed the courting of a bird, during the mating season, you will have a keen sense of the reality of the power employed. One of the birds, and it may be either a male or female, will be seen to actually "fascinate" or "charm" the one of the opposite sex, the latter lying still with quivering wings, and a helpless expression in its eyes. When compared with the attitude of the same bird, when charmed by a serpent, the resemblance will be striking.

SCIENTIFIC TESTIMONY.

I have before me a book written in 1847, which relates quite a number of instances of the operation of Mental Fascination among the lower animals. I will give you a few of them, condensed, and abbreviated.

Prof. Silliman is quoted as stating that one day, while crossing the Hudson River, at Catskill, he passed along a narrow road with the river on one side, and a steep bank, covered by bushes, on the other side. His attention was attracted by the sight of a number of birds, of a variety of species, who were flying forward and backward across the road, turning and wheeling in strange gyrations, and with noisy chirpings, seemingly centering over a particular point of the road. Upon examination the Professor found an enormous blacksnake, partly coiled, and partly erect, showing an appearance of great animation, with his eyes flashing like a brilliant diamond, and his tongue darting in and out. The snake was the center of the motion of the birds. The Professor adds that although the snake disappeared in the bushes, frightened at the approach of the men, still the birds seemed too dazed to escape, and perched on the near-by bushes, evidently awaiting the reappearance of their "charmer."

THE CHARMING BY SNAKES.

The same book relates an incident of a man in Pennsylvania, who saw a large blacksnake charming a bird. The bird described gradually decreasing circles around the snake, at the same time uttering piteous cries. It seemed almost ready to drop into the jaws of the snake, when the man drove off the latter, when the bird arose with a song of joy.

Another case is related of a ground-squirrel, which was observed running to-and-fro between a creek and a large tree a few yards distant. The squirrel's fur was badly ruffled, and he exhibited fright and distress. Investigation disclosed the head and neck of a rattlesnake, protruding from the hole of the tree, and *pointing directly at the squirrel.* The poor squirrel at last gave up the fight, and yielding to the fascination, laid himself down with his head very close to the snake's mouth. The snake then proceeded to swallow the squirrel, when his meal was interrupted with a cut of a carriage whip in the hands of the observer, and the squirrel, released from the spell, ran briskly away.

INTERESTING INSTANCES.

Dr. Good is quoted as having made quite a study of the curious fascinating power that rattlesnakes manifest over small animals, such as birds, squirrels, young hares, etc. He relates that these animals seem incapable of drawing their eyes away from those of the snake, and, although seemingly struggling to get away, they still gradually approach the snake, as though urged toward him, or attracted by a power superior to their natural instincts. He goes on to state that the animal creeps nearer and nearer, until at last it is drawn into the serpent's mouth, which has been open all the while to receive them. Dr. Barrow is quoted as relating many instances of this kind, known to peasants in all parts of the world. Valliant, the African traveler, tells of an instance in which he witnessed a shrike in the very act of being fascinated by a large snake at a distance, the fiery eyes and open mouth of which were gradually approaching the bird, the latter manifesting convulsive trembling and uttering piercing shrieks of distress. The traveler shot the snake, but upon picking up the bird, he found it dead—killed either by fear or the power of the serpent, or perhaps by the violent breaking of the spell. He measured the distance between the snake and the bird and found it to be three and one-half feet.

STRANGE STORIES.

A case is related in one of the early reports of the Philosophical Society, in which a mouse was put in a cage with a viper, by way of an experiment. The mouse at first seemed greatlv agitated, which state was followed by a condition of fascination, the mouse drawing nearer and nearer to the viper which remained motionless with distended jaws, and glistening eyes. The mouse, finally, actually entered the jaws of the viper, and was devoured.

Bruse, the African traveler, relates that the natives of an interior tribe seem to be protected by nature against the bite of scorpions and vipers. They are said to handle these creatures fearlessly, the latter seeming to be robbed of their power of resistance. He states that the creatures seem to sicken the moment they are touched by these natives, and are sometimes so exhausted by the invisible fascinating power that they perish shortly. He says, "I have constantly observed that however lively the viper was before, upon being seized by any of these barbarians, he seemed as if taken with sickness and feebleness, and frequently would shut his eyes, and would never turn his mouth toward the arm that held him."

"SNAKE CHARMER."

Personally, I have seen a somewhat similar case. When I was a boy, in Maryland, I knew of a farm-hand who was called a "snake-charmer." How he did it, I never could find out, but he would exert some kind of influence over all kinds of snakes, poisonous ones included, and would cause them to remain fascinated until with a quick movement he would grab them by the neck with his bare hands. This man generally carried a few pet snakes around with him for company. They seemed perfectly contented, and would poke their heads up from out of his pocket, in order to look at some one else with whom he might be talking. The negroes on the farm had a mortal terror of this man, and would walk a couple of miles rather than pass by his house.

FASCINATING FIERCE ANIMALS.

The power of charming animals, dogs and wild-beasts is undoubtedly possessed by some men, in varying degrees. And nearly everyone has known of men who could "charm" the wildest horses, as if by magic. I have read of some burglars who seemed able to quiet the most ferocious watch-dogs. The Swedish writer, Lindecrantz tells of certain natives of Lapland who are possessed of some process of charming dogs, to such an extent that they have been known to cow the most savage great-hound, causing him to fly from them with all the signs of abject fear. Many of my readers have seen, or heard of, the horse "whisperers" found in various parts of the country, who will shut themselves in a stable with a fierce horse, and by "whispering" to him will manage to tame him completely, and make him passive to their will.

CHARMED BY A SNAKE.

There are cases recorded in which men who have been "charmed" by a snake, have afterwards given in their experience. One of these cases relates that the man was walking in his garden when he suddenly came into the presence of a snake whose eyes gleamed in a peculiar manner. He found himself fascinated, as if by a spell, and unable to withdraw his eyes from those of the creature. The snake, he stated afterward, seemed to begin to increase immensely in size, and assumed, in rapid succession, a mixture of brilliant colors. He grew dizzy and would have fallen in the direction of the snake, had not his wife approached, throwing her arms about him, and breaking the spell. Another similar case is related, in which a man found his companion standing still on the road, with his eyes fixed intently upon those of a large rattlesnake which was regarding him fixedly with gleaming eyes, scintillating in its raised head. The man was leaning toward the snake, and would have fallen toward it in a few moments. He was crying, feebly, but piteously, "He will bite me! He will kill me!" "Sure, he will," replied his friend, "why don't you run away? Why are you staying here?" But the man seemed perfectly dazed, and distracted, and could not answer. The companion finally picked up a stick and struck at the snake, which glided away savagely. The fascinated man was sick for several hours afterward.

A PERSONAL EXPERIENCE.

When I was a boy, I had a somewhat similar experience, although not nearly so serious. Walking one day among a grove of trees belonging to my grandfather, I found myself standing staring intently at a snake about two feet long whose eyes glistened like large diamonds. In a moment I ceased to see anything but *those awful eyes* which glistened and displayed all the prismatic colors to my frightened glance. It lasted but a moment, however, for the snake glided away, seemingly as anxious to get away from me as I was to part company with him. I cannot say whether the spell would have been broken by me, if the snake had not moved away—perhaps it might, or perhaps not. All that I remember now, after the passage of thirty-five years or more, is that I did not seem to feel *fear* after the first shock, my feeling and emotion seemingly being that of *great wonder,* and *amazement* arising from *what I saw in those eyes.*

AN ELEMENTAL FORCE.

But I have said enough regarding the manifestation of Mental Fascination among the lower animals. There are many interesting instances of this sort, scattered through the pages of books on animal life, and nearly everyone who has lived in the woods, or among wild life knows of many cases illustrating this fact which have come under his own observation. I have mentioned these features of the subject merely for the purpose of showing you that we have to deal with a general natural principle which manifests throughout all life. This book has to deal with the manifestation of this force among men. But in closing this chapter, I would ask you to notice the resemblance between the manifestation of the force among the animals, on the one hand, and among mankind on the other.

The animals employ the force for two purposes, *i. e.*, the captivating of mates, and the capture of prey. And how do men and women use it? Along similar lines! Yes, I mean this, as startling as it may appear. For is not the use of fascination, in the direction of attracting the other sex akin to the sex-charming noticed among the birds and animals? And is not the use of fascination in the direction of influencing men and women along the lines of business, or personal interest, akin to the "charming" of prey by wild animals, serpents, etc.? You may see that evolution simply changes the form of use in this and other natural qualities, and power—the force or power remaining the same, under all of the changes. And, does it not become important for us to understand, study, and guard ourselves against the employment of such an elemental force as this, which manifests along all planes of life, from lowest to highest? I emphatically answer, Yes!

CHAPTER III.

THE STORY OF MENTAL FASCINATION.

The story of Mental Fascination runs along with the history of the human race, for it has always been known to man in some form. Coming to primitive man along with other inheritances from still lower forms, it was used from the beginning. Its earliest forms were similar to its employment by the lower animals, such as has been mentioned in the preceding chapter. The strong-willed of the race influenced and dominated the weaker-willed ones. Without understanding its laws, the strong-willed barbarians discovered that they possessed a strange power of inducing mental states among their weaker-willed companions, and were thus enabled to work their will upon them. Many of the leaders of barbarian races owe their positions of prominence and leadership to this law of mental induction.

THE MAGIC OF THE PRIESTS.

But along with the rise of leaders there was manifested a similar rise in power and influence of the priests. All races have had their priests, and have to-day. A priest is a man whose office is that of a mediator between men and their divinities—one who claims to represent the supernatural entities in their dealings with men—a religious, or spiritual "middle-man," as it were (I use this expression in all seriousness, and with no desire to sneer at the priestly offices, which have played an important part in the history of the race). The priests, not being occupied with warfare, or agriculture, and by reason of their support being contributed by the people, found plenty of time to "think," a somewhat rare privilege in the early days (and even in these times, for that matter). And, so, there gradually arose, among all peoples, a priestly caste that possessed the bulk of intelligence of the race. These priests soon began to recognize the importance of the Mental Forces, and they studied the underlying principles and laws of operation. This of course gave them an additional hold on the people, and a power over them. There seems to be no doubt but that even in the early days of the race, the priestly caste held a very wide knowledge of the laws and practice of Mental Fascination.

MYSTIC POWERS.

In the heart of Africa today, we find the Voodoo men, or Conjurers, or Medicine Men, well versed in the application of Mental Fascination. It was also known among the early American Indians, although their degenerated descendants seem to have lost the knowledge, except in a few instances. The power of the priesthood among primitive races, is based almost entirely upon some form of Mental Fascination. And, as we see the race ascending in the scale, so do we see the priests displaying a broader and fuller knowledge of the subject in question. The history of the Oriental races show that a full knowledge of the operation of Mental Fascination has been possessed by them for thousands of years. In the pictured stories of the Egyptians, the traces of which appear in their ruined temples and other buildings, we see that they understood the art perfectly. In ancient Persia and Chaldea, the art arose to great heights. In fact, among all of the advanced ancient races of men, we find an important place given to the subject before us.

THE ANCIENT MYSTERIES.

Among the Ancient Mysteries, and the various ceremonies of the temples, of the early races, we see many instances of the use of Mental Fascination. Back of the rites and ceremonies was always the same underlying principle of Mentative Induction. In the early use of the force, its employment was largely along the lines of healing, which phase of the subject does not concern us in this particular manual, although it belongs to the general subject of Mental

Magic. But still we read in the pages of early history of many instances of Mental Fascination, pure and simple. That which was afterward called Mesmerism, Hypnotism, etc., was well known to the ancients, and, in fact, some of the recorded results coming down to us from the past, have never been equalled by modern experimentors. Some of the feats of the modern Hindu magicians, or *fakirs,* which will be mentioned in detail, as we proceed, have never been equalled by Western hypnotists.

THE TALE OF THE MAGI.

As I have stated in Lesson IV, of "Mental Magic," the name "Magnet," given to the Lodestone, or natural magnet, was bestowed by the ancients because the observed properties of the lodestone resembled the mental power of the Magi or esoteric priesthood of ancient Persia and Medea. These priests were the "Magi," or "Wise Men," of the East, who had developed wonderful mentative powers, and who were known as wonder workers. The word "Magic" comes from the same source. When the attracting power and quality of induction, of the lodestone were noticed, it was remarked that the physical phenomena closely resembled the mental phenomena of the Magi, and, therefore, the lodestone was called "the Magian Stone," or "the Magic Stone," from which sprung the terms "Magnet" and "Magnetism."

As the centuries rolled by and the Western world had its attention called to the mysterious phenomena of Mesmerism, etc., in the Eighteenth Century, the public mind instinctively connected the phenomena with that of Magnetism, and the terms "Animal Magnetism," "Personal Magnetism," etc., came into general use. And these terms persist to this day, and we hear the terms "very magnetic"; "lacking magnetism"; "magnetic personality," etc., etc., as applied to people. And so history worked out an instance of the law of compensation. The Magnet, which took its name because its properties resembled the phenomena resulting from the use of Mentative Influence by the Magi, repaid the debt after many centuries, and served to give a name to mental manifestations resembling those of the Magi in the dim past. The Magnet gives back to the modern Magi the name it borrowed from the Magi of Ancient Persia. This is an interesting bit of Occult History little known to the general public.

JULIUS CAESAR'S FASCINATION.

Ancient history is full of instances of the operation of Mental Fascination among the people of the early days. It is related that Julius Caesar, while quite a young man, fell in with pirates near the Isle of Rhodes, who captured his ship, and took him prisoner. They held him for several weeks, while awaiting the ransom money being raised by his relatives. Plutarch writes that while the young Caesar was the captive of the pirates, he asserted his mastery over them to such an extent that he seemed a ruler rather than a prisoner. When he wished to rest or sleep, he forbade them to make any noise, and they obeyed him without question. He abused them and ordered them around like servants, and they did not seem able to disobey him. He did not hesitate to threaten them with death when he regained his liberty, and they did not resent it—and he afterward made good his threats.

THE MYSTIC POWER OF ALCIBIADES.

It is related of Alcibiades, the Athenian, that he once made a bet with some of the young Athenian nobles, that he would publicly box the ears of Hipponikos, a venerable and greatly respected citizen. Not only did he bet that he would do this thing, but he also claimed that he would afterward compel the old man to give him his favorite daughter in marriage. The day following, when Hipponikos came out, Alcibiades walked up to him and gave him a resounding box on the ears. The old man seemed dazed and bewildered and retired to his home. A great public outcry arose, and the young man seemed likely to fall a victim to the indignation of the citizens. But the next day Alcibiades went to the home of Hipponikos and, after making a pretence of baring his back for punishment, he managed to induce in the old man a feeling of good humor and mirth, and obtained his pardon and good-will, the latter increasing daily thereafter until finally he grew so devoted to the young man that he offered him the hand of his daughter in marriage, which was accepted. Any one who is acquainted with the recorded character of the Athenians will realize what a wonderful occurrence this was. It was a striking exhibition of Mental Fascination, without a question.

THE NAPOLEONIC CHARM.

All the great generals of history have possessed this quality. Caesar, Alexander the Great, Napoleon, Frederick the Great, and the modern Mystic-Warrior, Gen. Gordon, all managed their men in a mysterious and wonderful manner, so that their troops worshiped them as almost gods, and went to their death willingly and joyfully. The single instance of Napoleon, when he returned from Elba, and confronted the Bourbon army drawn up to capture him, should satisfy any one of the possession of the greatest Fascinating power by this wonderful man. You remember that the troops were drawn up confronting Napoleon, their muskets leveled at his breast in obedience to the command "Aim!" Napoleon, who was on foot, marched deliberately toward the troops, with measured tread, gazing directly into their eyes. Then the officers shouted, "Fire!" A single shot would have killed Napoleon, and would have brought to the man who fired it a fortune from the Bourbon King. *But not a man obeyed the order*, so completely were they under the spell of Napoleon's fascination. Instead of firing, they threw down their guns and ran joyfully toward the Corsican shouting, "*Vive l'Empereur!*" Their officers fled, and Napoleon, placing himself at the head of the troops, marched on to Paris. Other troops flocked to his standard at each point where he confronted them, although they had been sent out to capture or kill him. By the time the gates of Paris were reached, he was at the head of an immense army. The fascination manifested by this man was one of the marked instances of its possession of which we have any record. And it seems to endure to this day—almost a century after his death. The very mention of his name makes one's blood tingle.

MODERN EXAMPLES.

All great leaders of men, statesmen, orators, politicians, etc., have the power of Mental Fascination developed to a considerable degree. If you have ever come in contact with a man of this sort, you will always remember the impression he made upon you. Every man who knew James G. Blaine, will remember his "Personal Magnetism," of which so much was said during his lifetime. Anyone who heard the famous speech of Wm. J. Bryan, at the Chicago Convention, in which he made use of the famous expression:

"Thou shalt not press upon the brow of Labor the crown of thorns; thou shalt not crucify Mankind upon a Cross of Gold," needs no further proof of the reality of Mental Fascination.

Bryan was almost unknown to the majority of the delegates, and no thought of nominating him was entertained by them. But his "Magnetism" was so great that it swept the convention like a mighty tidal-wave, carrying all before it, and Bryan was carried around the hall on the shoulders of the delegates, who afterward made him their nominee for President. And although defeated twice, this man still possesses a wonderful fascination over hundreds of thousands of people in this country, who would rally around his standard at any time that he would sound the call. Henry Ward Beecher, at the great meeting in England, manifested the same power. The whole meeting was against him, and drowned his words by hoots, yells, and other noises. But Beecher looked them straight in the eye, and gradually *cowed* them into subjection, and then talked to them for two hours, and fairly carried the meeting by storm. He was but one man facing thousands of other men hostile to him, and determined to prevent him from speaking. But the single man won—by the power of his Mental Fascination, manifesting in the phase of WILL. It was not alone the words, in these cases—it was the WILL behind the words. The WILL is an *actual living force,* and is one of the two great phases, or poles, of Mental Fascination.

MESMER AND HIS WORK.

Coming down to the latter part of the Eighteenth Century and omitting all reference to the phenomena of Mental Fascination recorded in the Middle Ages, we reach what may be called the beginning of the revival of the subject among the Western peoples. I allude to the work of Frederick Anton Mesmer, a man who understood far more than he taught, but who was regarded as a charlatan and a trickster by the ignorant "learned men" of his day. Those who are informed regarding the secret history of Mesmer know that he was an occultist of no mean attainments, who was compelled to cloak his real teachings with popular theories and sensational phenomena, in order to gain the attention of the world, and also to escape religious persecutions.

Mesmer was born in 1734, and in 1775 began his work in Vienna by writing and teaching about a mysterious "universal fluid" which was able to control the wills of people, and also cure them of diseases, and which could be controlled and operated by man. He taught that there was a universal fluid which permeated everything, and was capable of receiving and communicating all kinds of motions and impressions. This "fluid" he thought acted immediately upon the nerves, in which it is embodied, and produced in the human body phenomena similar to that of the lodestone or magnet. He called this fluid "animal magnetism." He taught that this "magnetism" flowed rapidly from body to body; acted at a distance; was reflected by a mirror, like light, etc., etc. Mesmer attracted to himself great attention and great abuse. On the one hand he was sneered and scoffed at, and also driven out of the church for possessing "the power of the devil," and "witchcraft." But on the other hand, he gathered around him a body of supporters and students. He was "investigated" by a Royal Commission, and by scientific bodies, with varying results. The coming of the French Revolution interfered with the general interest in the subject for a number of years. Mesmer's followers adhered to his general lines of theory and practice, with unimportant additions or changes.

THE ABBE FARIA.

In 1814, the *Abbe Faria* attracted much interest in Paris. His theories were different from those of Mesmer, inasmuch as he claimed that the "sleep" produced by Mesmer and his followers was not the result of any outside force, but was caused by the patient himself. For a number of years a spirited contest was waged between the two schools of "Mesmerists," and much bad feeling was developed.

BRAID AND "HYPNOTISM."

Then came James Braid, the Manchester surgeon, who proceeded to tear down the accepted theories, substituting one of his own. Braid may be called the father of "Hypnotism," the term being first employed in connection with his work. His theory was that there was no such thing as "animal magnetism," but the phenomena obtained by Mesmer and his followers was caused by a physiological condition brought about by physical means, such as fixing the eyes, rigidity of the muscles, etc. Braid made some very important contributions to the knowledge on the subject, although, of course, all that he wrote or taught was colored by his own particular theories. Braid regarded the "hypnotic sleep" produced by his methods, as the necessary condition and cause of the phenomena of "animal magnetism." Braid's writings brought the subject before the attention of physicians, who had up to his time avoided it as "unprofessional," etc., and a series of investigations by medical men in France and Germany were begun, and have continued up to this time. The result of such investigation has been the placing of the subject upon a "scientific" basis.

LIEBAULT AND SUGGESTION.

Dr. Liebault, of the School of Nancy, France, first brought into prominence the theory of "Suggestion," which has since found so many followers. Dr. Bernheim, a pupil of Liebault, in his work "Suggestive Therapeutics," carried his teacher's theories on still further. The theory of Suggestion, as taught by Liebault and Bernheim, was that the cause of the phenomena of "mesmerism" and "animal magnetism," etc., lay in the "Verbal Suggestion," or "Verbal Command" of the Hypnotist to the subject, given and received while the subject was in a deep hypnotic sleep. This "hypnotic sleep" was considered to be an essential and fundamental pre-requisite of the phenomena. It was all "SLEEP," with the teachers, students, and investigators at that day—and the majority of them are still under the spell of the old teachings.

BERNHEIM'S MISTAKE.

As an instance of how near a man may come to a thing, and still miss it, I may mention that Bernheim has recorded that in *rare cases,* where the conditions were exceptionally favorable, he could obtain results *even when the subject was not asleep.* But he missed his opportunity of following up this promising lead, and to the end he proceeded upon the belief and theory that the "hypnotic sleep" was a necessary precedent to the phenomena obtained. He endeavored to produce the condition of "deep sleep," or "profound hypnosis" believing that the same was a necessary condition for "suggestibility." The very word "Hypnosis" arises from the Greek word meaning "to lull to sleep," so you can see how deeply this idea of "sleep" was and is, among hypnotists. Remember this, always, please—HYPNOSIS MEANS A CONDITION OF SLEEP, so never use the word in any other way. Mental Fascination is *not* Hypnosis, although Hypnosis is a form of application of Mental Fascination.

THE NEW SCHOOL.

During the past ten years or so there has arisen a new school of investigators of the phenomena of "Mesmerism," etc. This new school proceeds upon the theory that the "hypnotic sleep" is merely an incident, and that all the phenomena obtained by the earlier authorities is possible without the production of the sleep condition. In other words, SLEEP IS NOT A NECESSARY CONDITION OF SUGGESTIBILITY. This brings the new school of the Suggestionists very near to the occult idea of "Mental Fascination," although there are some radical differences, as I shall show in a moment. In 1884 Dr. Bremand announced that had made the discovery that there is a "fourth hypnotic (?) state," which he called "Fascination," which left the subject in full consciousness of his surroundings, and remembrance of what had taken place. If Bremand had only had the courage to omit the fetich-word "hypnotic" from his statement, he would have founded a new school. But he didn't! The German, Froman, wrote a large book on the subject of "Fascination," which he defined as *"Hypnotism, without the putting to sleep."*

THE TRUTH ABOUT SUGGESTION.

Some of the best work along the "without-sleep hypnotism" (?) has been done by American experimentors and investigators (principally physicians), nearly all of whom believe that "Suggestion" is the explanation of the whole thing, and that there is no such thing as the passage of "Mental Currents." These "Suggestionists" hold that the subject acts upon the Command and Suggestion, and does what he is told—and that that is all there is to it. The "Suggestible Condition" to them means a condition in which the subject yields up his whole "attention" to the operator, and thus becomes "suggestible," the degrees varying with the temperament, etc., of the subject.

While the "Suggestionists" believe that Suggestion is the whole explanation and cause, I hold that it is *but one of the methods* of producing the effects, and that back of Suggestion is the Induction of the Mental State by the Suggestor, as I have stated in my work on "Mental Magic," and as I shall bring out in the present manual.

PERSONAL MAGNETISM.

Along with the new theories of "Suggestion without Sleep," there has arisen a great interest in "Personal

Magnetism," during the past few years. There has been much written on the subject—some good and some ridiculous, and some between the two extremes. The laws of the subject are being studied by the thinking public. There has been a great revival in the interest in Occultism, which together with the various phases of Mental Science, Theosophy, New Thought, and kindred subjects, has attracted the attention of a large portion of the public to the general subject of Mental Magic, and to the special subject of Mental Fascination, in particular. And this manual is written in response to the present demand for definite information on the subject.

I feel sure that I will be able to show you that the Law of Mentative Energy, in its operation along the line of Mentative Currents, as stated in my book on "Mental Magic," will account for all the phenomena mentioned above in the History of the General Subject, as well as many other forms. I believe that I can bring it all under the definition of "The action of a Mental Force that powerfully influences the imagination, desire, or will of another"—which is my definition of "Mental Fascination."

CHAPTER IV.

THE RECONCILIATION.

In my last chapter I have shown you the opposing theories of the various schools which have investigated and experimented along the lines of Mental Fascination, under some of its many names. All of these schools obtained results, notwithstanding their varying and diametrically opposite theories—*the same kind of results,* remember. And more than this they all obtained these results in very much the same way, when we come to examine the essence of the procedure, after discarding the forms added to fit in with the particular theories of the practitioner.

A NEW SYNTHESIS.

I believe that all the opposing theories of the schools may be reconciled by a new synthesis—that of Mentative Energy with its incidental phenomena of Mentative Induction, as set forth in my "Mental Magic," and further expounded in this little manual of which this chapter is a part. I believe that theories so far divergent as Mesmer's Universal Magnetic Fluid—

Abbe Faria's Sleep—Braid's Hypnotism—Bovee Dods' Electro-Biology—Liebault's Suggestion—Bernheim's Suggestion—the later Suggestion-without-Sleep—Bremand's Fascination—and the various other theories advanced since the time of Mesmer—can be reconciled and harmonized by a careful application of the theory of Mentative Induction as advanced in my work on "Mental Magic."

And I believe that all the phenomena obtained by any and all of the above schools; as well as the phenomena of the Ancient Fascinators; and the phenomena known as "Personal Magnetism," "Charming," "Personal Influence," "Magnetic Personality," etc., etc., of ancient and modern times, may be accounted for by the same theory. And so this chapter shall be devoted to the reconciliation of the various old theories with this basic principle of Mentative Induction.

MESMER EXPLAINED.

Let us first examine the real facts underlying Mesmer's theory of the Universal Magnetic Fluid. Mesmer taught that there existed a peculiar subtle fluid, "magnetic" in its nature, which was diffused throughout all space; which permeated everything, and which was capable of receiving and communicating all sorts of motions and impressions. He taught that this "fluid" flowed freely from one body to another, acted at a distance, and could be reflected by a mirror, etc.

He did not explain what this "fluid" was, except that it produced "magnetic" effects, and must therefore be magnetic in its nature. He proved that he could produce effects, and he gave out a theory to fit in with the facts, and that was within the comprehension of the people of his time.

Now, let us apply the idea of Universal Mentative Energy, with its incidental phenomena of Mentative Induction, to Mesmer's theory, and see how easily the reconciliation is effected. The Mentative Energy, like Mesmer's "fluid," is Universal; is diffused through all space; permeates everything. Like the "fluid" it apparently passes from body to body and communicates impressions, etc. But we now know that the Energy is transmitted in waves or vibrations which reproduce the original feeling by Mentative Induction in the second person. There is no necessity for the flowing "fluid" any more than there is for an "electric fluid" flowing over the wires, or through the air. The "fluid" idea has been superseded by the "wave" idea, in both physics and metaphysics.

THE NATURE OF THE "MAGNETIC FLUID."

We may readily see that this "magnetic fluid" theory of Mesmer may be explained by the theory of Mentative Energy, and Mentative Induction. There is no "magnetic" fluid. The Energy is Mental in nature and operation and the phenomena arising therefrom is

Mentative also. Mesmer sought for his answer in physics—but we find it in metaphysics. The force is not physical—it is mental.

All the phenomena obtained by Mesmer, and his followers, may be accounted for by the theory of Mentative Energy, and Mentative Induction. The Mental States of the Mesmerist may be communicated to his "subject" by waves of Mentative Energy, and a corresponding feeling or Mental State is induced by Mentative Induction. As we shall see as we proceed, the "sleep" of the Mesmerists and Hypnotists is merely an induced condition arising from the desire in the mind of the operator, accompanied by the Suggestion on his part.

FARIA EXPLAINED.

The theory of *Abbe Faria*, that the "sleep" condition was not the result of any outside force, but arose from within the patient himself, is also reconciled by the theory of Mentative Energy and Induction. Of course the "sleep" arises from within the patient himself—but it is *induced* by the waves of Mentative Energy of the operator, accompanied by his active Suggestions.

BRAID RECONCILED.

Braid's theory is also reconciled. He held that the phenomena was of a physical nature, rather than a mental, and that it was a reflex physical action arising from fixing the eyes, rigidity of the muscles, etc. His hypnotic sleep was undoubtedly heightened by his practice of tiring the eyes and muscles, on the same principle that one is tired mentally by unusual exercise of the eyes, as in the cases of visiting an art gallery, museum, strange city, etc., and that the power of resistance is thereby weakened, and one is far more likely to then accept suggestions of mentative waves. How many of us have felt mentally "done out" after visiting a museum, or after witnessing a long parade, or after sitting through a modern circus performance, with its three rings going at one time? And who does not remember how many foolish things he had done at times when he was "too tuckered out" to object to the suggestions and influences of those around him.

A DANGER SIGNAL.

Many a girl has gone to her ruin by the subtle suggestions and influence of some male scoundrel, directed toward her after an evening of the "show," or circus or after a day of sight-seeing in a strange city. I tell you, friends, that in such cases the Will becomes tired by overuse arising from unaccustomed tasks, and it becomes "woozy" and incapable of resisting the attacks upon it. As I have told you in my larger work, beware of all suggestions, etc., when in a tired state. Make a habit of saying "No!" to attempts to make you commit yourself at such times. Wait until you feel fresh and strong, and the Will is able to attend to its business for you. Many a man has said "Yes!" to his sorrow, to propositions advanced to him when he was tired by the day's work, and his Will was weak and unable to resist. I cannot say this to you too often, and have therefore dragged it in again at this place. There is a great psychological principle involved in this point, and you will do well to fasten it in your memory.

Braid's theory may be reconciled to the idea of Mentative Energy and Induction, when we see that his eye fixation, and muscular rigidity is merely the means of producing a "suggestible condition," that is to say, a condition in which suggestions are more readily accepted, and mentative currents more readily received—in both cases the tired Will allowing the outside influence to enter.

SUGGESTION EXPLAINED.

The theories of "Suggestion" are not contrary to those of Mentative Energy and Induction, when properly understood. The facts of the Suggestionists are undoubted, but they make the mistake of ignoring the Mental States of the Suggestionist. They think that their effects are produced by Suggestion alone, and forget the Mental State behind the Suggestion which is the real motive force. If their theories be true, why is it that two men using the same words of Suggestion, upon the same subject, produce varying degrees of effect? It is because the Mental States or Dynamic Mentation of the two men vary in quality and degree.

The Suggestionist thinks that he is merely directing his "Suggestion" by words, etc., toward the subject, but all the time he is pouring out a current of Mentative Energy which rapidly induces the desired mental state in the subject. The best Suggestionists are those who have acquired the "Suggestive Manner" which is developed by the exercise of authoritative utterances and commands, the physical appearance, manner, and tones arising from a reflection of the Mental State within. I have seen this in the case of one of America's most celebrated Suggestionists, a prominent physician and scientist, with whom I was associated in magazine and other work in the years 1900-01. I have seen the doctor giving the most powerful suggestions at one of his classes or clinics—so powerful were the emanations of Mentative Energy, or currents of the same, that the members of the class could distinctly "feel" the same, and at times could almost "see" them. And yet the doctor, who was wedded to his particular theories of Suggestion pure and simple, after such a wonderful manifestation, would calmly inform his class that it "was nothing but Suggestion—nothing more to it." And he believed it—but hundreds who attended his classes went away more firmly convinced than ever that there was "something more to it," and that there was a cause behind his "Suggestions." The theory of Suggestion is all right—but what lies back of Suggestion? What gives the Suggestion its force? Of what inner and invisible thing is the Suggestion the visible and outward sign? MENTATIVE ENERGY!

INHARMONY HARMONIZED.

And my theory of Mentative Energy and Induction may be reconciled with the theories of the later Suggestionists—including those who still adhere to the "sleep" delusion, as well as those who have advanced beyond it. And it explains all the phenomena of the ancients, with their religious and mystic rites. The phenomena of Charming, Fascination, Personal Magnetism, Personal Influence, etc., is all embraced under the theory advanced in this work, and my larger work which preceded it.

As we proceed with this work we shall see the Mentative Energy, and Mentative Induction in actual active operation in these various phases of phenomena, but I trust that this chapter will have shown you that there is one principle underlying all of the various theories and phenomena, and that the facts of Mentative Energy, and the operation of the same in its phenomenal incident of Mentative Induction are sufficient to include and cover all of the varying manfestations of the Force observable under the disguises of the conflicting theories of the various schools and cults. There is but one underlying cause, and that is MENTATIVE ENERGY. There is but one underlying law of the operation of this Force in the direction of affecting other minds, and that Law is Mentative Induction, either direct, *i. e.*, by Mentative Currents; or indirect, *i. e.*, by Suggestion; or (as is generally the case) by both combined.

CHAPTER V.

THE RATIONALE OF FASCINATION.

In this chapter I shall proceed to lay before you the "rationale" of Fascination, that is, an exposition of the principles of its operation. While the phenomena of Fascination extends over a very wide area or field, there is still to be found a certain unity of principle of operation underlying all of the forms and phases. From this point of view, we may speak of the "Science of Fascination," as well as of "The Philosophy of Fascination."

THE FUNDAMENTAL PRINCIPLE.

The fundamental principle of the operation of the Mental Phenomena known as Fascination is found in the theory of Mentative Induction, as stated in my work on "*Mental Magic,*" and which is briefly stated in the first chapter of the present book. This theory, you will remember, holds that each Individual Mind is a Center of Mentative Energy, and that the Mentative Energy of an Individual Mind may be, and is, transmitted from one person to another by means of

Mentative Waves or Currents; (3) that these Mentative Currents or Waves tend to "induce" in the minds of other persons the emotions or feelings existing in the Mental States of the person sending out the Waves or Currents.

In this connection, we must also remember that there are two Mental Poles, known as the Motive and Emotive Poles, respectively. The Motive Pole manifesting as Will-Power, and the Emotive Pole manifesting as Desire-Force. Desire-Force acts in the direction of drawing, pulling, attracting, luring, coaxing, charming, etc.; while Will-Power acts in the direction of compelling, forcing, driving, impelling, commanding, demanding, etc. Desire-Force *always draws its object toward itself;* while Will-Power always *overpowers and compels its object,* generally in the sense of driving it into action.

MENTATIVE INDUCTION.

This Mentative Induction acts along similar lines to the "induction" of Electricity and Magnetism, that is, it sets up similar states in the object affected. And the resemblance is even still further marked when we consider that the phenomena of Electricity closely resemble the action of the Will, inasmuch as both tend to *drive outward* in the form of an Impelling Force; and that the phenomena of Magnetism resemble the action of Desire, inasmuch as both tend to ***draw inward*** in the form of an Attracting Energy.

AN INTERESTING QUESTION.

In this connection, however, I would direct the attention of the student to one fact concerning the effect of induced states, which some have failed to grasp in my teachings in my work on Mental Magic. The matter may be stated by the inquiry of a student of the last mentioned work, who inquires, as follows: "Please inform me how it is that an induced mental state *reproduces the original mental state of the Mentator* in the following case: a man *desires* to have another perform a certain act, and sends a mentative current which acts by induction on the mind of the second person, setting up an induced mental state therein. The second person then performs the act desired by the first person. Now, if the induced mental state was the same as the original one, would not the second party simply also *desire* that the first party should do the act, just as the first party desired that the second should do it? But it does not work so, for the second party does not so desire, but instead merely desires to do just what the first party desired him to do—that is he feels within himself a desire *to do* that which the first party desires *shall be done*. It seems to me that the induced state is really the *opposite* of the original state. Please set me straight on this?"

THE ANSWER.

I am very glad to have the opportunity to "set straight" my students on this point. A little careful examination will show that both states are similar. For instance, A desires that B shall *do* a certain thing, and induces a *similar state* in B. The induced state produces in B a like desire that the things *shall be done,* and he proceeds to do it. No opposite action here, is there? The essence of the DESIRE *in both cases* is the same, namely, *that the thing shall be done.* The expression of the feeling of the two persons in the case, as (1) "I Desire that You Shall Do," and (2) "I Desire to Do," respectively, are merely the personal forms of expression, and not the essence of the Desire or Feeling. The Desire or Feeling, in *its real essence* is, *"I desire this thing done."* And both hold *the same Desire,* A holding the original Desire or Feeling, and B the induced Desire or Feeling. Think this over a little, until you see the point.

Induced Will acts in the same way as the above mentioned instance of the action of induced Desire. Of course, in all cases of the action of Desire the Will is also called into operation. In the above cited case it works as follows: A feels the Desire to have the thing done, and so his Will is called into operation to concentrate the Mentative Currents, and to project them to a focussed point in the mind of B; then B, feeling the induced Desire that the thing shall be done, awakens his Will *and does the thing.* Do you see this also? You had better fix this process firmly in your minds, for it is the key to the operation of the principle of Fascination, and other Mentative Phenomena.

MAKING ANOTHER "FEEL-LIKE" DOING.

Now to get back to the first principle, which is *that one person may make a second person FEEL LIKE DOING a thing that the first person wishes to have done.* That is the thing in a nutshell. And in the degree that the second person so *feels* like doing the thing, so will be the degree of Desire and Will induced in him, and consequently *so will be the likelihood of his actually doing it.* You see the matter of "FEELING-LIKE" is at the bottom of it all. And this being so, it is readily seen that if one is able to *induce* a state of "feeling-like" in another, he has the secret of the control of the other person's actions. Now this is the BASIS OF MENTAL FASCINATION!

Now let us see how this principle works out in a case of Mesmerism, or Hypnotism, so called, which after all is but a phase of Mental Fascination, governed by the above mentioned principle. I prefer the term Mesmerism for several reasons, among them being the fact that it is a recognition of Mesmer, its discoverer, or re-discoverer; and also the fact that Hypnotism means "sleep," while Mesmerism covers the whole phenomena, in both its waking or sleep conditions.

A CASE OF MESMERISM.

Well, let us suppose a case of Mesmerism. The Mesmerist, whom I will call the "operator," faces the "subject." The operator assumes a positive state of mind, his Will Power being active and concentrated, practice having improved him along these lines. The subject naturally assumes a negative mental state, opening his Emotive Mental Pole to the influence of the Mind or Will of the operator, and allowing his Motive Mental Pole to remain quiescent or relaxed. That is to say, he opens his Desire mind to the influence of the operator, and lets his Will remain inactive and relaxed. The operator Desires and Wills that the subject be influenced, and the subject agrees, consciously or unconsciously, to be so influenced—one Wills, and the other "is willing" (which latter paradoxical expression means that he is *not Willing*). The operator naturally asserts his positivity, while the subject assumes a decided state of Negativity—one asserts a Supremacy of Will, and the other submits. I would call your attention to the fact that there is no physical compulsion, or influence, in the matter—it is all a matter of Mentation! And both parties fully recognize the reality of the phenomenon.

THE SILENT CONFLICT.

The above relative mental state of the two persons is apparent in a greater or lesser degree whenever two persons meet. One is always stronger Mentatively than the other, and a silent conflict ensues from which one or the other emerges a victor—and the result is recognized and acquiesced in by both victor and vanquished. Ordinarily, however, the distinction is not nearly so marked or great as in the case of a strong Mesmerist and his negative "subject," the latter having probably been trained in Negativity by repeated trials and experiments in private and in public. For know you, that even as Positivity may be cultivated, developed and strengthened by practice and actual performance, so (alas!) may Negativity be encouraged, developed, and made habitual by a continued practice of "giving in" to the Will of another, or others,—it is all a matter of habit.

POSITIVE AND NEGATIVE.

It will be seen at once that given a subject and operator bearing the stated degrees of relative Positivity and Negativity, the subject will have a tendency to accept and obey the wishes and commands of the operator with a minimum degree of resistance. The operator will strongly wish the subject to feel in a certain way, and to act upon the feeling. To accomplish this result he will concentrate his Desire by his

Will, and then direct a combined and focussed attack on the mind of the subject. He is likely to call Suggestion to his aid, in the attack, for by so doing he is able to obtain an additional advantage, for a Suggestion (as I have stated in my work on Mental Magic) is a "Physical Agent inducing Mental States" —or "an outward and visible sign of an inward feeling or mental state," which tends to induce a similar feeling in the mind of accepting the Suggestion.

THE SUGGESTIVE COMMAND.

The operator gives the subject the "Suggestion by Command," and in accordance with the phase of Suggestion known as "Suggestion through Obedience" (see my work on "Mental Magic") the subject obeys. It must not be forgotten, however, that *the Suggestion is merely the outward symbol of the inward mental state of the operator*, and becomes effective only by reason of this fact. The operator throws his intensified Desire-force and Will-power into the Suggestion, and receives an effect along the line of the three-fold activity. With his Will he produces a dual effect, *i. e.*, (1) he captivates the Desire of the subject, and induces in it the desired "feeling-like" state; (2) he takes captive the Will of the subject, and subjugates it to his own. And, at the same time, by his Desire he also produces a dual effect, *i. e.*, (1) he induces a similar desire in the mind of the subject by mentative-waves, or currents, and (2) he allures, or seduces the Will of the subject by the strength of his Desire. The result of this "combined attack" causes the *mind of the subject* to act as follows, which adds a third dual-effect to the operation, *i. e.,* (1) the subject's Desire (being induced as stated by the operator) acts to influence his own Will, thus making the latter fall in with the induced Desire; (2) the subject's Will (controlled as stated by the operator) acts upon his own Desire, thus making the latter fall in with the seduced Will.

It must be remembered that the three mental operations above mentioned are concurrent, that is, they act at the same time, and exercise joint action and control upon the mind of the subject. And neither the operator nor the subject are necessarily conscious of there being three dual-actions under way. The operator simply Desires and Wills, with or without Suggestion; while the subject simply "feels-like" (as before stated) and accepts the Suggestion if one is given, without recognizing the various mental operations going on to produce the "feeling-like." The detailed explanation may make the operation seem complicated —while in reality it appears to both the operator and subject as quite a simple matter, indeed.

THE "DAY-DREAM STATE."

The above process is the same, whether the operator merely produces the simplest result upon the subject, or whether he secures the most remarkable and startling exhibitions of the control of one mind by another. The principle of operation is the same in all cases. With sleep, or without sleep, it is the same. In fact, as we shall see, the very "sleep" condition is produced just as are the other effects, and its production merely tends to produce a "day-dream" state in the subject, and thus makes him act in a day-dreamlike manner, with appropriate illusions. Sleep phenomena are merely one of the "side-issues" of Mesmerism, when the true principle is understood.

HABIT AND REPETITION.

In our consideration of the operation of Mesmerism we must not forget the part that *habit* and *repetition* play in the matter. For instance, the operator may be able to produce only the simplest effects at first trial; but at each subsequent trial, in which he gains more and more control over the subject, and a greater acquiescence and degree of obedience, he is able to obtain a still more marked effect. If you will read the remarks on "Suggestion by Repetition" in my work on "Mental Magic" (page 120) you will realize the awful force of repetition and habit, as well as the power of repeated statement. This psychological fact is like the operation of the wedge—admit the thin edge, and each additional blow drives it further in. This works along the lines of both good and evil, remember

—the wise use it to their own strengthening, while the foolish allow it to be their undoing. *Beware of the thin edge of the wedge of undesirable habits of thought and action.*

A PSYCHOLOGICAL LAW.

The Mesmerist understands well, often too well, the nature and results of the above mentioned psychological law. He has found out by experience that although it may be difficult to control a subject the first time, it will be easier the next; and so on and on, until perfect control is obtained. And, knowing this, he bends his endeavors to inserting the very thinnest edge of the wedge, understanding that in this he has his hardest task before him. And, alas, how many of us know that this same principle is in operation in every day life, although seemingly having nothing to do with Mesmerism. How many of us are able to regret the day of the entry of the thin edge of the wedge.

Another point to be remembered is that the subject who is under a fair degree of control does not feel as if he were obeying the commands or wishes of the operator alone. That is, not in the main. It is true that he instinctively obeys the command of the Suggestion, just as a horse quickens his gait when spoken to, or a soldier acts quickly in obedience to orders, etc., etc. But the motive for the action, or feeling, seems to come *from within* himself to a great degree. It has the force and effect of an *instinctive action proceeding along sub-conscious lines.* He seems to *want to do* the thing of his own accord. This is the dangerous feature.

This, then, in a general way, is the rationale of Mental Fascination as shown in its phase of Mesmerism, and its corresponding exhibitions along less pronounced lines. If you will acquaint yourselves with these principles of operation, you will have a grasp on the whole subject. In our next chapter we shall have a view of the Mental States of Operator and Subject, which will throw additional light upon the subject before us.

CHAPTER VI.

IMPRESSIONABILITY.

In the last chapter I laid before you an exposition of the principles of the operation of Mental Fascination, particularly in its phases of Mesmerism. The student who has followed what I have said therein has seen that there must, of necessity, be a marked difference in the degree of Impressionability, or Receptivity to Mentative Induction, manifested by the operator and subject respectively in order that the pronounced phenomena may be manifested. But this difference of degree of Impressionability is manifested by all men and women. Between the one extreme point in the scale of Impressionability to the other extreme there are many degrees—and each person has his or her own degree, subject, of course, to change by development.

MAGNETIC POSITIVITY.

I would like to quote from my work on "Mental Magic," illustrating this last mentioned point. I have said therein: "I do not mean that the degree of Magnetic Positivity is fixed permanently in either person, for the contrary is the case. One of the persons, who is really the stronger, usually, may be weaker at that particular moment, owing to his Will being fatigued, or by reason of his having relaxed his Will-Power, as is often the case. And in such case the defeated one may be the victor at the last encounter, or may even rally his energies a moment later, and thus turn the tables. One may have a strong Will in moments of activity, and yet in moments of passivity he may relax it very much. And this is a still more important fact: one may so increase his Will-Power that he will be able to completely dominate those who formerly over-mastered, and even over-awed, him. All of us know of instances of this kind in our own personal experience."

THE TWO EXTREMES.

At the extreme point of Mentative Positivity are the wonderfully strong-willed men who are "natural leaders" and managers. At the extreme Negative Mentative point are those people who are moved by every passing suggestion or mental current with which they may come in contact—those impressionable people who seem to live in the emotional plane of their being, and who are always open to outside influences, and are like weather-cocks moved by every passing breeze. These people are really the reflection of the thoughts, desires and wills of others—the last person who catches their attention being the "right one" to follow. You all know the type, don't you?

I do not mean by this that only persons naturally weak-willed may be mesmerized. But I do say that when strong-willed people allow themselves to be mesmerized they must relax their Wills and become passive or negative to the operator, else there will be no result gained. A strong-willed man may voluntarily relax and become negative in order to be mesmerized. I have seen this done in many cases, although I have always urged against it, for I consider it inadvisable for one to surrender his Will in this way, even for the purpose of scientific investigation. I am sure that I would not do so myself, and therefore I cannot approve of the practice on the part of others.

THE "ARTISTIC TEMPERAMENT."

Then again, I have known people of a highly developed "artistic temperament," such as actors, poets, artists, writers, and others who possessed strong Wills, to allow themselves to become very "impressionable" by reason of their active imaginations. That is to say, they would allow themselves to be so carried away with the idea of being impressed that they would "throw themselves into the part" of the mesmerized subject, and *actually mesmerize themselves,* although allowing the operator to take the credit. This last explanation will throw light on a phase of the phenomena that apparently presents an exception to the rule, but which when viewed in the light of the above explanation, may be seen to come strictly within the rule of Positivity and Negativity.

A MESMERIST'S TRICK.

Public performers of mesmerism, when they meet with an imaginative subject whose will is too strong to subdue, often begin to bend their efforts toward arousing the imagination of the person and thus causing him to become passive and in a subjective condition of "acting out" the part suggested by the operator. In such cases there is no "conflict of wills" whatever, but, on the contrary, the subject *wills* to act out the part and becomes the *partner* of the mesmerist, instead of his opponent. The subject in such cases mesmerizes himself, and voluntarily allows himself to be led by the suggestions of the operator so long as the suggestions are not contrary to the subject's own interests. This "actor instinct" is very strong in some people, and this self-mesmerism is far more common than people imagine. It is seen on the stage, and among speakers and writers.

MESMERIC SUBJECTS.

Even many of the best mesmeric subjects who travel around with the professional mesmerists are of this last mentioned class to a certain degree. They are able to throw themselves into the parts, and play them well, so long as they are not adversely affected thereby. They are far different beings from the weak-willed, flabby creatures that are so often seen following around after the professional mesmerists. The imaginative "professional subject" is alive to his own interests, and as a somewhat cynical friend of mine, who had made a close study of the subject, once said, even the most obedient subject of this class would utterly fail to act upon the suggestion of his powerful operator to effect that the subject consent to a reduction of his weekly wages paid by the operator—even though the "deep stage" of hypnotic sleep be produced.

"DON'T SURRENDER YOUR WILL."

But I consider that even this imaginative class of subjects are unwise in allowing themselves to be guided and governed by the suggestions and commands of any operator, for I believe that even such a habit is injurious to the Will. The Will is a precious thing and should not be prostituted in this way. I cannot urge this too strongly upon my students. I say to them: "Surrender your Will into no one's keeping." Regard it as a woman should her Virtue, and allow no one to take liberties with it.

WHO CAN EXERT FASCINATION?

The average person possessing self-confidence and force can, and does, exert Mental Fascination over others with whom he comes in contact, although it requires a developed Will to become an expert in this line of mental work. Besides this, there is undoubtedly a certain "knack" and technique about the work, which is acquired by practice, although some seem to have it considerably developed naturally. There are geniuses in Fascination as well as in art—and there are others who have acquired the mastery in both by careful practice and determination.

THE REQUISITE FOR FASCINATION.

In considering the qualities that go to make up the person in whom Mental Fascination is likely to be strongly developed, I may mention the following:

(1) *Physical Well-Being;* for there is a certain strength about a man or woman in strong, robust health, that must be taken into consideration. It is true that some persons not physically well, but unhealthy, have exercised strong powers of Fascination, but this was *in spite of* their lack of physical health, and owing to a strong Will which allowed them to master even this obstacle. But, all else being equal, there is a power about a strong, healthy, vigorous person that makes itself felt.

(2) *Belief in One's Self;* for without this no one

manifests Positivity. Believe in your own power and ability, and you impress others with the same belief. Confidence is contagious. Cultivate the "I Can and I Will."

(3) *Poise;* for the calm, well-poised, imperturbable man has an enormous advantage over one lacking these qualities. The man who meets any emergency without "losing his head" has something about him that makes him looked up to as a natural leader—he has one of the qualities of Positivity. Cultivate the Calm, Masterful mood.

(4) *Fearlessness;* for Fear is the most negative emotion in the being of man. Fearlessness is a most Positive quality, just as Fear is the most Negative. Cultivate the "I Do—I Dare."

(5) *Concentration;* for this "one-pointedness" focuses the Will-Power upon the object. Do one thing at a time, and do it with all the power that there is in you.

(6) *Fixity of Purpose;* for you must learn to know what you want to do, and then "stick to it" until it is done. Cultivate the Bull-dog quality—it is needed.

To those who recognize the need of the above mentioned qualities, but who lack them, I would recommend the careful study and determined application of the principles of "*Mental Architecture,*" as stated in my Seventh Lesson in my work on "*Mental Magic,*" in which the matter is gone into in detail, with exercises, etc.

NONSENSE EXPOSED.

There has been much nonsense written about "who make good subjects," etc., in works upon Mesmerism, Hypnotism, etc., and many amusing rules for the determination of the degree of impressionability have been given by many writers. Some say that brunettes are the most impressionable, while others assert that blondes yield more readily, etc., etc.; but the experienced investigator laughs at such distinctions. Some consider that women make the best subjects, while others assert that men really are more readily influenced. My own opinion is that the percentage is about the same in both sexes. Then, again, one must remember that the degrees of "impressionability" are *relative*. For instance, A may be positive to B, while B may be positive to C, and so on to the end of the alphabet. And, using the same illustration, M is negative to L, though positive to N. Do you see this?

A LIE NAILED.

Some writers have tried to make people believe that only "strong-minded" people may be mesmerized, and give as a proof thereof the fact that idiots and insane people are almost immune from hypnotic and mesmeric influence. This is a favorite argument of the professional hypnotists, who use it in order to put at ease their subjects, or possible subjects, who might not wish to appear as "weak-minded" people. The truth is that the reason that the above classes are exempt is because (1) the idiots have little or no power of attention, and are like mere machines, and consequently cannot be induced to pay attention long enough to be mesmerized, but all advanced students of Mental Influence know that idiots, as well as animals may be influenced by Mental Vibrations, or Mental Waves, etc., by "treatments"; (2) insane people are usually carried away with a "fixed idea," or delusion, and are, in fact, practically in a state akin to that produced by hypnotic or mesmeric process to a marked degree. Their minds are centered on the delusion and cannot be taken off it. If the attraction could be removed the patient would no longer be insane; and although the "sleep condition" cannot well be induced in insane patients, still the best authorities know that such people often yield to strong suggestions, and mental treatments, to a certain degree, so that the rule does not always hold.

IMPRESSIONABLE PEOPLE.

The class of people who yield most readily to Mesmeric influence (outside of the sub-class of imaginative people mentioned a few pages further back) are those who have not manifested their Will, Determination and Self-Reliance very much. People who have led a life in which implicit obedience, or reliance, upon others, have been cultivated—these are the people who are most impressionable. They have not used their Wills, and are more readily ruled by the Wills of others, or through their Emotions. As I have said in my larger work: "The degree of response to Suggestion by Command is to be observed in the highest degree among those who have always depended upon others for orders, or instruction, and have not had to use their own wits and resources in life. Unskilled laborers, and the sons of rich men who have had some one to think for them, often belong to this class. These people seem to want someone else to do their thinking for them, even in the smallest event of their lives, and are most impressionable along the proper lines. Then the degree of Positivity rises as we consider the people who have had to do things for themselves, and who have not depended so much upon others. Positivity is the greatest among people who have had the ordering of others to do, or who have had to depend upon their own resources, and their own wits, in getting through life. The men of marked Initiative have scarcely a trace of this form of suggestibility. 'Initiative,' you know, is a term for 'doing things without being told'—using one's own wits, and resources, and WILL." The above applies equally to the subject of "impressionability" to mesmeric influence. And what does it all mean when it is "boiled down"? Just this—that the degree of "impressionability" depends upon the degree of the lack of Will Development. The word WILL is the keynote! And this in spite of all the talk, twaddle and nonsense written and spoken by those who are interested in having the people appreciate "the wonderful virtue (?) of Hypnotism."

THE "MOB SPIRIT."

The reason that mobs allow themselves to be influenced is because they surrender their Individuality, and Individual Will, and allow it to become merged with the Wills of others, until a "mob Will" is created, which represents the average of the crowd, the weaker wills diluting the strength of the whole. When this mess of mingled and weakened will is properly mixed it remains in a dazed and excited condition until some Individual springs to the front—some leader of men who has held on to his Individual Will—and impresses his Will upon the more negative Will of the crowd, and the mob accepts his suggestions and follows like sheep, or mesmerized subjects, and does his bidding until some other leader catches its attention and interest.

EMOTIONABILITY.

There is another phase of mentality that has its bearing upon the degree of impressionability. I refer to the quality known as "emotionability." An emotional person is one who more readily throws off the influence of his own Will and Reason and gives himself up to the play of the emotional side of his nature. Such a person is more impressionable than one who is not so emotional, but whose Will is really no stronger. The reason is that by his mental habits he has accustomed himself to "open up" his Emotive Pole of Mentality to outside influences and allowing his Motive Pole to remain inactive. He allows his "feelings" to rule him, instead of ruling his feelings—he allows his Emotional Nature to usurp the throne of his Will, the latter being relegated to second place. And the consequence is that his Emotive nature has become more open to unresisted, outside influences and impressions and responds more readily to the same—it has acquired the "impressionable" habit. Do you see? This last explanation will throw some light on the fact that certain races of people are far more "impressionable" than others—they are more Emotiona' that's all.

WHO IS AN "IMPRESSIONABLE"?

In the following chapters I shall use the term *"impressionable"* as a noun, designating a person who is sufficiently impressionable to respond to the influence of a mesmerist or hypnotist to a greater or lesser degree. These "impressionables" are comparatively easily impressed by the Mentative Force, and Suggestions of the Experimenter along these lines. Please remember the sense in which I shall use the term. Later on I shall use the term *"hyper-impressionable"* as a noun, indicating a person excessively, or abnormally impressible by mesmeric influence. The latter class will be further described in the proper place in the book.

Let me give you a fanciful illustration of the subject of impressionability. It will form the subject of our next chapter, which will be entitled "The Fable of the Mentative Couple." It will explain not only the matter of response to mesmeric influence, but will also throw light on the exercise of Personal Mental Influence that is going on around us in everyday life, all the time, everywhere. You will have a much clearer idea of the matter after reading this Fable—and you will also be much more on your guard because of the lesson taught therein. Do not fail to read it carefully and seek for the secret contained within its lines.

CHAPTER VII.

THE FABLE OF THE MENTATIVE COUPLE.

Once upon a time there lived in the land of Mentalvania, in a wonderful building called The Mentative Castle, a Man and a Woman, called "The Mentative Couple." They were Happy though Married. They Lived in Harmony, because they were Useful to One Another, and neither was complete without the presence of the Other—and neither did his or her Best Work, unless the Other was present and assisting.

VOLOS AND EMOTIONE.

Well, now, the Man was called "Volos" (which is the same as the English name "Will"), and the Woman was called "Emotione," which in the language of that country meant something like a combination of Emotion, Desire and Imagination.

THE TWO NATURES.

Now, the Chronicles inform us that these Two People had natures entirely different from each other, as has been said. We are told that Volos was of a stern, inflexible, strong, positive nature; apt to stick to a thing once begun; full of the "will-to-live" and "vitality;" full of determination and spirit with a strong dash of the "let-me-alone" and "get out of my way" in his make-up; with a taste for meeting difficulties and overcoming obstacles; with a goodly degree of habit of reaching out and taking hold of what Emotione wanted and needed; and a powerful lot of Self Respect and Self Reliance in him. He was apt to be firm although his firmness was not the stubbornness of the mule, and his general keynote was Strength. He was a good warrior and defender of his castle. But Emotione was of an entirely different type, temperament, and character. She was most impressionable, imaginative, emotional, credulous, fanciful, full of desire, curious, sympathetic and easily persuaded. While Volos was all Willing and Thinking, Emotione was all Feeling.

FIRE AND WATER.

Volos was a Strong Character, but lacked certain qualities that make for Success—but these qualities Emotione possessed, and she supplied the deficiency in Volos. Volos had to "figure out" everything, while Emotione had Intuition, and jumped at a conclusion in a way remarkable to Volos, who couldn't understand the process at all. When he would ask Emotione for an explanation, she would say, lightly, "Oh, just *because!*" which answer would often provoke profane and irreverent discourse on the part of Volos. But, nevertheless, he learned to respect these "becauses" of Emotione, and found that they helped him in his business. Emotione would dream out things, and see things a long way ahead, and then Volos would proceed to put these plans into operation. Volos couldn't see very far ahead of his nose, while Emotione could see miles beyond, and years ahead. And besides this faculty of Mental Imagery that came in so useful in Volos' business, Emotione also possessed a burning and ardent Desire for Things, which she managed to communicate to Volos, thereby causing him to get out and Do Things that otherwise he would never have dreamed of doing. Emotione was like Fire, and Volos like Water. The Water would hold the Fire in check, but at the same time the Fire would heat up the Water and the result would be the Steam of Action. And, so, you see these two—this Mentative Couple—formed a fine co-partnership, and prospered mightily.

ENTER THE TEMPTER.

But, alas! the Tempter entered Eden—and the Attractive Stranger meandered in the direction of the Mentative Castle, and when he reached there trouble occurred. And this is what happened:

THE UNGUARDED CASTLE.

One day Volos was absent from the Castle, being engaged in some arduous enterprise. And consequently the Castle was Unguarded. Volos had provided against this by instructing Emotione that she was to keep the Castle Gate closed tight, when he was away from home, and never to gaze without in his absence, for there was some mysterious danger lurking without when he was away. Emotione had faithfully followed the directions of her liege lord, although her womanly curiosity was piqued thereat. Many the time she had heard strange knockings at the Castle Gate, but she heeded them not, and even refrained from looking out of the little peep-hole in the Gate—though this last was much against her inclination, for she could see no harm in "Just Looking."

THE FASCINATING STRANGER.

But, to return to our tale, this particular day when Volos was absent from Home, her curiosity was too much for Emotione when she heard the strange knockings at the Gate. And, breaking her rule, she ventured to peep without. Looking down she saw a most attractive stranger, with a fascinating smile on his lips. He looked almost as strong as Volos, but he seemed to have a Dash of the Woman in him, besides. He had the Strength, but also the Charm that Emotione recognized as being a part of her own nature. "Ah," sighed Emotione, "here is a Man who can Understand me." The Fascinating Stranger smiled sweetly, and looking her in the eyes, masterfully asked to be admitted. "No, no," replied Emotione, "I cannot let you in, for Volos told me not to." "Ah, fair lady," said the Stranger softly, "Volos means all right, but he is rather old-fogyish, and behind the times. He does not 'Understand,' as do you and I. Pray, let me in." And, like Mother Eve, Emotione took the bait.

"WHEN THE CAT'S AWAY," ETC.

Well, to make a long story short, when Volos came home he found that Emotione had subscribed to a set of "Villeveaux Modern Art," a beautiful work issued by the De Luxe Bros. of Fifth Avenue, to be issued in 824 weekly parts, at the nominal price of $5 a part—739 parts of which were already out, and would be Delivered Shortly. She had also given a number of Side Orders for Manifold Wares, which had dazzled her untrained and unguarded Fancy. Volos cried aloud to the Gods of his Land—but it was too late, the contracts had been signed.

WORSE AND MORE OF IT.

But, that was but the beginning. Volos did not understand just what was the matter, and contented himself with scolding Emotione, whereat she wept bitterly. But the poison went on with its deadly work. And when Volos again was absent from home, the habit reasserted itself, and when the Fascinating Stranger again called at the Castle, he was admitted. And when Volos returned, he found the Castle furnished from dungeon to watch-tower with costly rugs, and furniture, and various other articles, bought from "Morganstern's Popular Installment House," at $1,000 down and $100 per week. He also found that the Castle had been Lightning-Rodded from ground to turret, on each wing, tower, and annex; and that Notes, containing a law-proof, judgment-confessed clause, had been given in exchange therefor. And then Volos swore by the Beard of Mars, the War-God, that he would have no more of this—He would Remain at Home thereafter And he Did.

But the Subtle Stranger was Onto the Game, in all of its Details. And this is how he Played it on Volos, even though the latter Remained at Home.

HOW VOLOS MADE A MISTAKE.

A few days after Volos had determined to Remain at Home, there came a band of mountebanks, singing, dancing, and performing juggling tricks. Volos sat on the great stone beside the open Castle Gate, and his Attention was attracted by the sounds and sights. Faster the dancers whirled—louder beat the drums—sweeter grew the singing—more bewildering grew the feats of jugglery—until poor Volos forgot all about the open Castle Gate, so rapt was he at the strange sights, sounds, dances, and feats of jugglery. Then one of the mountebank gang (who. was really the Attractive Stranger disguised in motley array) slipped, unseen, past Volos, and in a moment was engaged in eager conversation with the impressionable Emotione.

Volos watched the crowd until it moved away, and then entering the Castle, and closing the Gate behind him, was confronted by Emotione, in tears, for she dreaded the coming storm. "Alack a-day, woe is me," she cried, "I am again in trouble, O, Volos, my liege lord! I have just ordered from the Fascinating Stranger, who slipped past you at the Gate, a Baby-Grand, Self-playing, Automatic, Liquid-Air valved, Radium Carburetter, Harpsichord, upon which I may play for you all classes of Music, ranging from Vogner's *Gotterdammerung* to the popular rag-time air entitled "Kiss Yo' Babe Good-Bye!" with feeling, depth of expression, and soulful understanding, according to the words of the Fascinating Stranger who took my order."

"Gadzooks!" ejaculated Volos, "Fain would I cry aloud the name of that production of Vogner's just mentioned by thee. And by my Halidom, e'en shalt thou soon be singing to me the words of that rag-time melody just quoted by thy false red lips! Zounds! Of a Truth I have been Stung Again by that Fascinating Stranger. I must gaze no more upon these Fleeting Scenes of Merriment and Amazement, lest I be again decorated with the Asses' Ears. Aha! Volos is himself again, and the next time the Fascinating Stranger appears upon the scene, he shall be smitten hip and thigh with my trusty battle-axe, and my snickersee shall pierce his foul carcass!"

But, alas! even once more was poor Volos deceived and trifled with—once more was poor Emotione Fascinated by the Stranger. And it came about in this way.

HIS LAST UNDOING.

On the day of his last undoing, Volos sat on the open step, in front of the narrowly opened Castle Door. "No man shall pass me now," cried he. But Fate willed otherwise. For as he sat there, there approached many people who took seat upon the steps before the gate, and engaged Volos in long heated, and wearisome discourses regarding the Outlook for the Crops; the Presidential Campaign; the Japanese Question; Race Suicide; the New Theology; How Old was Ann; the Problem of the Final Outcome of the Collision between the Irresistible Force and the Immovable Body; the Canals on Mars; what Roosevelt Will Do when his Term expires; and many other weighty, interesting, and fascinating topics of general interest. Most agreeable were these visitors, and most considerate of Volos' feelings were they. And although they seemed to differ from him at the beginning of each argument, still they courteously allowed him to convince them inch by inch, until they finally acknowledged that he was Invincible in Argument, and Invulnerable in Logic. " 'Tis passing Strange," quoth Volos, "but nevertheless 'tis true—that *I always find myself on the Right Side of Every Question.* And the wonder grows when they all admit it in the end. Verily, am I developing into a Wise Guy!"

THE LAST STRAW.

And, pondering thus, he fell sweetly asleep from the rigor of the disputes; the flattering attentions shown him; the joy of the victory; and the exceeding amount of attention and interest he had expended, for Human Nature has its limitations, even in the case of one so Strong as Volos. And while he slumbered, the Fascinating Stranger (who was really the leader of the Argumentative Visiting Committee), crept into the house and unloaded upon Emotione a choice collection of Gilt-edged Mining Stock (pure *gilt,* all the way through in fact); a bunch of Flying-Machine Bonds, and a 5,000 Donkey-Power, Vestibuled, Drawing Room, Observation Car, Automobile called the "Yellow Peril." And when Volos discovered what had happened he wept aloud, crying bitterly, "Oddsbones; S'death—of a cert am I the Baron E. Z. Mark."

And thereupon he sent for the Wise Man who dwelt in the next barony.

THE WISE MAN CALLED IN.

The Wise Man came, and after hearing the story said: "My children, yours is a sad case, but matters may be adjusted without a visit to Sioux Falls, and without the raising of the question of Alimony. The trouble is as follows:

VOLOS WITHOUT EMOTIONE.

"Volos, without Emotione, has no Desire or incentive to Do Things. He has no wants to satisfy, and therefore Does Nothing. He needs Emotione to supply the Desire. And without her he has no Feeling—he is nothing but a hard-shell clam. Therefore he needs her to supply the Feeling, for verily, and of a truth, Feeling is the spice of Life. And without her he has no Imagination, and cannot see beyond the end of his nose—and what is life without Imagination? Gadzooks, one might as well be a mummy!

EMOTIONE WITHOUT VOLOS.

"And on the other hand, Emotione without Volos, is a consuming fire of Desire; an unrestrained Imagination; an Intuitive Faculty degenerated into the basest superstition, most deplorable credulity, and the idlest Fancy. Volos has no Desire, Emotion, or Imagination of his own—and Emotione has no Will of her own.

IN UNION IS THERE STRENGTH.

"Verily, cannot it be seen by all that this Couple needs One Another the worst way? Each, alone, is but an Incomplete Half. United they stand—divided they Fall. In Union alone is there Strength for Them.

THE DANGER OF SEPARATION.

"And more than this, each, without the other, falls a prey to the wiles of some Fascinating Stranger. We have seen how Emotione was fascinated and controlled by the Will of the Stranger who gained access to the Castle. But I have also seen (by my Magic Art) that when Volos was away from home on 'important business,' without having Emotione along to keep him straight, he fell a victim to the wiles of the Desire and Imagination of a Fair Stranger across the river, and did her bidding, and used his Will to perform her tasks, instead of those desired by his own Emotione. Verily, art these people quits with one another and should now begin over again. True it is that Harmony will be theirs only when they Are Together.

THE SECRET OF THE UNDOING.

"And this is the Secret of the undoing of Emotione. Without the Will of Volos to protect her, direct her, and advise her, Emotione allowed her Desire, Imagination, and Emotion to run wild and unrestrained. And so she became so impressionable as to allow herself to be mastered by the Will of the Stranger, who took advantage of the same and gathered to himself many Choice Orders for Things. And even when Volos sat by the door watching the players, dancers, and jugglers, his ATTENTION was so centered on what he saw, that the Fascinating Stranger slipped through the Gate—it was even as if Volos had been absent from Home. And, again, when Volos allowed himself to become engaged in weighty discourse with the Visiting Committee, and used up his Energy and Force in Argument and Dispute with them—and when he permitted himself to be "jollied" into a false security by these United Brethren of the Blarney-Stone—he relaxed his Vigilance, and allowed himself to become tired, drowsy and sleepy, and so fell into a doze at his post, and the Stranger again entered and took Emotione's Orders for Goods.

THE WISE MAN'S REMEDY.

"And this then is the Remedy (as my successor, Lawson of Boston, will say in the centuries to follow)—this is THE REMEDY. Each person of this Mentative Couple must stick close to the other. Volos must have no 'important business' across the river, which will allow Emotione to be without a protector and advisor. And Emotione must stick close to Volos, and satisfy her curiosity, imagination, emotion, and desire, by setting him to work out things for her —to do things dreamed of by her—to get her things she desires—to express the things felt by her. This is the Secret of Success, dear Mentative Couple—Mutual Work by Desire and Will, working in Unison and Harmony—each faithful to the other—each guarding the other from the Fascinating Strangers that beset each when separated. Now, then Children, GET TO WORK!"

And saying this, the Wise Man vanished from sight.

THE MORAL.

And the Moral of this Fable of The Mentative Couple is this: That the Mind of every Man and Woman is a Mentative Castle, wherein dwells a Volos and an Emotione. And what happened to the Couple in the Fable, may happen, and does happen, to many in everyday life. The Will, straying from home, and paying attention to other attractions leaves the Castle unguarded, and the Fascinating Stranger enters. And, again, the Will has its Attention distracted by passing objects of interest, and forgets the Castle Door. And again, the Will allows itself to be fatigued, tired, and jollied by useless argument, and talk, and cogitation, at the instigation of the Designing Fascinating Stranger, and the latter slips past the Gate. And in each case, inside the Gate is Emotione unprotected, and innocent, true to her own nature, credulous, imaginative, fanciful, desireful, and emotional—is it any wonder that she "orders goods" that are not wanted by the family? And the Remedy of the Wise Man as given to the Mentative Couple may be, and should be, applied by every Man and Woman in his or her Mental Castle. And this then is the Moral of the Fable.

CHAPTER VIII.

EXPERIMENTAL FASCINATION.

In this work I shall give the student an idea of the methods of conducting experimental work in that phase of Fascination which has been called "Mental Impression," etc., following the lines of the best investigators and experimenters in America and Europe. My reason for so doing is that the student may have a thorough idea of the practical work, even though he may not wish to conduct such experiments in person. I think that everyone should be made acquainted with these things as a matter of knowledge, and also for purposes of the self-protection which arises from an understanding of the subject.

STARTLING PHENOMENA EXPLAINED.

I also desire to satisfy the careful student and investigator that the feats, tests and phenomena which have heretofore been regarded by the general public as inseparably connected with mesmerism, hypnotism and "sleep-conditions" may be reproduced without the aid of "sleep-conditions," and without the hocus-pocus of the public performer. The entire phenomena of mesmerism, hypnotism, etc., may be produced by simple, scientific methods along the line of Mental Fascination, by means of Mentative Induction, without any attempt to produce "sleep" as a necessary precedent condition. When this matter is thoroughly understood by the public the glamor and sensationalism of public mesmeric and hypnotic performances will vanish, and the subject will receive the scientific consideration that it merits. But at the same time people will begin to realize the mighty power of the Mental Influence that is capable of producing such startling manifestations in a waking state, and will seek to guard themselves against the abuse of the power.

HYPNOTIC PERFORMANCES CONDEMNED.

It should be almost unnecessary for me to add that I have no sympathy with the public performances of that phase of Mental Impression known as "Hypnotism, Mesmerism," etc., in which subjects are made to go through all sorts of foolish and absurd performances. Outside of my objection to people surrendering their Will to another in this way I feel that such exhibitions are lacking in feeling, good taste and often in decency. To say the least, it is making "horse-play" of a scientific phenomenon. I have nothing in sympathy with such manifestations or exhibitions, and shall speak of them in this work only to condemn the methods employed.

SCIENTIFIC METHODS.

In my remarks, and instruction, along the line of entific methods along the lines of the best authorities upon the subject, and in accordance with the rules observed at the best-conducted experiments of such authorities, at which experiments I have frequently been present. I wish my students to place themselves in a scientific attitude of mind, just as if they were attending lectures on the subject at some leading university in its scientific course. The subject is a strictly scientific one and should be approached, considered and investigated only in accordance with the scientific spirit of investigation. It is not a matter for fun (?), or idle amusement. I trust that I have made my position on this point sufficiently clear to all, so that there may be no misunderstanding regarding the same.

THE IMPORTANCE OF THE KNOWLEDGE.

I do not advise *all* of my students to engage in this experimental work, for there is no necessity for them so doing. What I am really trying to do is to acquaint them with the methods used in these experiments, and the results obtained. In this way they may acquire an extended knowledge of the subject, which will enable them to really "understand" the different phases, and prevent them from entertaining erroneous ideas concerning the matter. This knowledge will also enable them to detect any symptoms of an attempt to use this force upon them in everyday life. When a person becomes acquainted with the true inwardness of a thing, so that he recognizes it whenever he sees it, there is little danger of his falling into error regarding it. The knowing of a thing is half the battle of repulsing it.

And with this understanding, and with this explanation, I shall now proceed to describe the work in Experimental Fascination, now being performed by scientific investigators in the colleges and other places in this country and in Europe.

FAVORABLE ENVIRONMENTS.

The investigator of Experimental Fascination soon learns that certain environmental conditions have a marked effect on the degree of success attending his experiments. And, accordingly, he endeavors to surround his experiments with the best conditions possible, as indicated by his experience. A knowledge of these conditions is an important thing for an investigator and experimenter along these lines.

DESIRABLE CONDITIONS.

The investigator finds that he can obtain much better results when his experiments are conducted in a quiet place, the atmosphere of which is conducive to calm, undisturbed, peaceful mental states. This atmosphere affects both operator and subject, allowing the former to concentrate his mind and the latter to give his full attention and to rest in a passive mental state. It is well if the experiments be conducted in a room remote from the street, and as far as possible apart from the rest of the house, so that noises of either cannot well penetrate. The experimenter should also take measures to prevent interruption, for the latter will interfere with his concentration, and the subject's attention.

SENSE IMPRESSIONS.

The best experimenters see that their experimenting room is furnished plainly, having no pictures or decorations, etc., calculated to attract the subject's attention. A soft carpet which will deaden the sound of footsteps is advisable. I have seen some experimenters even go so far as to place rubber tips, or cushions, on the feet of the chairs, tables, etc., in the experimenting room, in order to obviate sudden noises. The room should be kept at a comfortable temperature, neither to warm nor too cold, as either extreme will make the subject uncomfortable and less able to give his full attention to the experimenter. I have heard of cold rooms, draughts, etc., interfering with the best conducted experiments, and every experimenter is aware of the fact that a close, sultry day will interfere seriously with his experiments. Care should be taken to avoid a glare of light in the room. Shades of soft greens or blues are advised, and these same colors should be used in the decorations of the rooms by the experimenter who wishes to obtain the best results. Remember the expression, "a dim, religious light," and you will get the right idea.

PSYCHOLOGICAL EFFECTS.

Some experimenters burn a little incense in the room before the experiment is performed, the same having a tendency to quiet the nerves and impart a feeling of restfulness to those in the room. You will notice that the conditions that tend to produce the most successful results in these experiments are the same that the ceremonial churches of all races have adopted in their services, etc. This fact needs but bare mention to the thinker. It is well known that soft, quiet religious music will produce a psychological condition in which persons become quite impressionable, and some of the French psychologists have taken advantage of this fact. The whole theory rests upon the production of a feeling of "ease" in the subject. Consequently, it is scarcely necessary to add that the chairs should be very "comfortable" and "easy."

THE ROOM OF A LEADING SUGGESTIONIST.

I may conclude these remarks upon desirable conditions, by quoting from an article for a magazine written by myself about seven years ago, under a pseudonym. The article described the experimenting room of a leading American suggestionist, at a series of experiments conducted before a class of investigators and students, at which I had been present. I think that the description will convey to your minds the ideal conditions for experiments along these lines. I said in the article: "The room is well ventilated and lighted, although there is an absence of glare. It is remarkably quiet and free from disturbing sounds and sights, the air of seclusion and remoteness from the scenes without being very marked. The impression grows upon one and reminds him of the interior of some quiet old rural chapel, on a summer afternoon, when all around seems to indicate the lack of existence of an outside world, save the occasional breeze faintly fanning the cheek, and some muffled sound seeming to come from some far distant point, and perhaps the droning of some stray bumblebee that had chanced to float in the open door. The semi-religious air is heightened by the 'dim religious light,' and by the voice of the experimenter as he gives the repeated suggestions to the patient, in the same monotonous tone, encouraging and hopeful, and at times reminding one of an earnest prayer. The surroundings, the stillness, the tone of the operator, the reclining position of the patient, all give the strongest suggestion of quiet, calm, peace, ease and rest, freedom from care and worry, relief from pain and trouble,—Nirvana. The influence of these suggestive surroundings is distinctly felt by the visitor, and he also unconsciously assumes the role of the attendant at the chapel. The writer was told by some of the patients that they soon become totally oblivious of the presence of the class, and are to all intents and purposes, alone with the operator, with no other thoughts than the suggestions being made to them." I might add that the suggestions given to the patients at the beginning of the treatment were calculated to increase the desired mental state of rest, calm, and quiet.

HOW TO DETERMINE "IMPRESSIONABILITY."

The first thing that the experimenter does is to determine the degree of impressionability of the "*impressionable.*" There are a number of ways to determine this. One of the methods that have been found the most effective is to have the "*impressionable*" partially extend his left hand and arm, until an easy position is obtained. Then have him hold the hand with palm downward, and then raise, or elevate, the third finger of that hand (generally known as the "ring-finger") holding the other fingers steady, and down, on a level with the palm. Then tell him that you will proceed to WILL that he shall feel a *tingling sensation* in the finger, which feeling will increase gradually, and will then begin to extend up the hand, and wrist and then up the arm to the shoulder. Tell him that the feeling will be faint at first, but that it will begin to "tingle" more and more in a few moments, and then it will extend in the manner stated. Then concentrate your own mind on the feeling you desire to produce in him, and WILL strongly that it be produced. After a moment ask him whether he does not feel the faint tingling sensation—but *note this,* ask him in such a way as to give him the positive suggestion that he *does*—this way, for instance: "You feel the tingling already, don't you." This form of question is really a suggestion, for you state the thing before asking the question. When you say *"don't* you," emphasize the *"don't,"* sharply and positively. You will find that the sensation is perceived in a moment or two, in a large percentage of cases, and in many cases the more pronounced results are obtained. The degree of sensation produced determines the degree of impressionability of the person tested. When you conclude the test, in each case, be sure to take the subject's hand, grasping it firmly, and shaking it gently, saying: "Your hand is *all right* now—*all right,"* emphasizing the words "all right," and saying them firmly, and positively. Always say these things with an air of conviction, and assurance—for there is a great suggestive quality in such tones.

TESTING A ROOMFUL OF PEOPLE.

If you are testing a number of people—a roomful, for instance, you should pass rapidly over the number to be tested until you have finished. You may test the whole roomful at one time, as above, if you desire. Do not act as if you were attaching much importance to the test, telling them that you are "merely testing them for impressionability," etc. But when you have finished, you will know just the degree of impressionability of each person in the room, and you will thereby be enabled to select the most impressionable for the next test.

IMPRESSING THE SUBJECT.

Having selected the desired number of "*impressionables*," pick out one of them, and ask him to stand up before you, looking you straight in the eye (see direction for acquiring the "Magnetic Gaze" in a later chapter), saying to him, in a quiet but firm, positive tone words to this effect: "Now give me your *entire attention.* I wish you to fix your attention firmly upon me and what I am saying, for in this way only can the best results be obtained. You must forget everything and everybody else in the room, and must hear only my voice and feel my thoughts. Make yourself perfectly *receptive and passive* to my thoughts and words. There must seem to be no one else here but you and I. You must see no one else; must hear no other voice; must think no other thoughts, but Mine. Give me your full attention now, and open yourself to the inflow of my Thought." Talk to him a few moments in this strain, and then say: "*That's right*, now you are giving me your *full attention*—you are now *feeling my Thought*—all is going well," etc., etc., in an encouraging tone, in the same spirit as you would to a child who was trying to perform some task under your direction.

INDUCING RELAXATION.

Instruct him to relax all of his muscles—to take the tension off of them. Tell him that in so doing he will "draw his Will away from his muscles," which is just about what really happens. If he seems to be slow at grasping the idea, give him a practical illustration of "relaxation," by lifting one of his hands and then letting it drop. If it does not drop freely, then he has *not* relaxed. Try him until he learns just what "relaxation" means. This practice will bring about a state of passivity which will tend toward success in your experiment.

EXERCISES IN RELAXATION.

It is of the greatest importance that the subject of the experiments be brought into a passive condition of mind. And the best way to induce this desired condition is to bring about *a passive condition of body*, for the latter will have a reflex action on the mind, according to well-established laws. The following exercises will aid you to bring about the relaxed condition, preparatory to your psychological experiments:

EXERCISES.—Instruct the subject to withdraw his Will from his right hand, making it perfectly "limber," so that he may swing it loosely from his wrist. Then have him so swing it backward and forward. Repeat with the left hand. Then try with both hands at the same time. Then have him impart to the hands a "twisting" motion, to and fro, from the wrist, of course letting them twist about limply.

Then have him withdraw the Will from his arms, and then shake and twist them about from the shoulder, like a pair of empty coat-sleeves.

Then lift his arms up above his head, and allow them to fall like a dead weight to his sides—the falling must be occasioned by the weight of the arm, and not aided by his Will—his Will must be withdrawn entirely.

The above exercises may be varied and amplified, as found desirable.

PUTTING SUBJECTS AT EASE.

Some of the best experimenters take considerable time in "putting at ease" the persons who offer themselves as subjects for psychological experiments, and at the same time they bring about the desired state of relaxation. They realize the distaste and fear that anything like hypnotism inspires in the minds of people, owing to the public performances thereof, and they avoid any suggestion of similar conditions. They generally begin by talking of the value of relaxation, and how few people are able to relax their muscles. Then they illustrate the matter by showing the subjects how few of them are able to relax easily. This leads to the trying of the above mentioned Relaxation Exercise, or similar ones, which, as you will see in a moment, leads directly to the first real test of Mental Induction and Suggestion, which is known as the "Falling Forward Test," and which is one of the simplest tests known to the psychological laboratory. From that test to others, it is merely a matter of successive steps. So the experimenter really begins his work with the process of "putting the subject at ease," and training him in relaxation. In this connection I would say that very few people know how to "relax," and some teaching is necessary in the majority of cases. The above exercises should be sufficient.

THE PRIMARY TEST.

After instructing the subject in relaxation, say to him: "Now, look me straight in the eyes, and let my Thought act through you. You are feeling an inclination to *fall forward*—FALL FORWARD—FALL FORWARD toward me! Do not fight it, but yield to it—yield to it, I say! I will catch you as you fall. Now fall forward toward me slowly. That's it, you are leaning a little now. Come on, come on, *come on now,* this way, *this way.* NOW!" Extend your two hands, one on each side of his head, but a little in front of him, so that he can see the palms of your hands which should face each other. Then as you repeat the suggestions mentioned above, draw your hands slowly away from him, as if you were "drawing" him by some physical power. This is a strong suggestion, which will render him more susceptible to your Will. The more reality you throw into the "acting out" this "drawing" the more strength will you put into your Willing, and the more readily will he obey.

USING THE WILL.

While saying these words look intently into his eyes, and WILL that he fall forward. In a moment he will begin to sway forward a little, and if you keep up the concentrated WILL, and suggestions he will fall forward toward you. Be ready for him, and catch him with your hands. This test is far more simple than would seem from reading the description of it, and is capable of being produced in a large percentage of cases, where the persons will allow their minds to become passive to yours. Where there seems to be a resistance, tell the person to "hold the thought" that he is inclining forward toward you. Some find it easier to feel the "falling forward sensation" with their eyes closed, than with them open. With others the reverse is true.

REVERSING THE TEST.

After you have succeeded in this experiment, stand behind the person about one yard, and concentrate your gaze upon a point at the base of the skull, that is, where the neck joins the head. Then tell him that he will experience a *"falling backward"* sensation, just as he did before in the "falling-forward" test. Be sure to tell him that you will catch him when he falls, etc., in order to reassure him. Use the same tones, etc., as in the falling-forward test, except that you substitute the word "backward" for "forward." In a few moments you will obtain the same result as in the falling-forward.

Both of the above experiments are among the easiest tests known to experimenters, but they are important inasmuch as they serve to inspire confidence in himself, in the mind of the experimenter, and a passive confidence in the mind of the *"impressionable."* Then it is always well to begin by these easy tests, and then work up by degrees to the more difficult ones, even upon subsequent occasions.

THE "FASTENED PALM" TEST.

The next test may be as follows: Tell the "*impressionable*" to place the palm of his hand upon your own, allowing it to rest there a few moments, withdrawing all of his Will from his hand, and leaving it perfectly relaxed and like a "dead weight." Then tell him that you are going to *fasten his hand to yours* by Thought. Then, looking him straight in the eyes, say, in a strong, firm, positive tone: "Now you CAN'T take your hand away—you CAN'T, I say—try, *but you CAN'T.* Try, try, try—you Can't, you Can't, you CAN'T, I Say," etc. Always accent the word "Can't" in these experiments, for that is the word you wish to emphasize and drive home in his mind. And you must, of course, accompany your words by the thought, "You CAN'T"—you must WILL that he cannot. Remove the impression by saying, "All right, now—all right."

THE "LOCKED FINGERS" TEST.

Your next test is that of *fastening his own hands together.* This is accomplished by getting him to "lock" the fingers of his two hands together, holding them as tight together as he is able to do, using his Will actively in so doing. Then say to him, "Now do not resist me, but remain as you are. Now, you CAN'T unloose your hands—you CAN'T, I say, you CAN'T—try, but you CAN'T," etc., etc., at the same time concentrating your gaze and WILL upon his hands, thus holding them together. It may help you in the beginning to hold his hands together with your own, at the first, and then gradually loosen your own, until they are entirely away from his hands, repeating your suggestions meanwhile. Remove the impression as previously instructed.

THE "CLENCHED FIST" TEST.

Your next test may be that of *preventing him from unclenching his fist.* Proceed as in the last test, telling him to clench his fist together as tight as he can, and then you must say to him: "Now you CAN'T unclench it—you CAN'T, I say, etc." It will be some time before he can get his fist unclenched. Remove the impression.

ROTATING HANDS TEST.

The next test may be that of *making him rotate his hands.* Proceed by telling him to relax his hands, somewhat, but begin to rotate them around each other in an outward direction. Then say to him, "Faster, *faster,* FASTER, FASTER—as fast as you can." Then when his hands are rotating rapidly, say to him: "Now you CAN'T stop them—you CAN'T, I say—try, but you CAN'T, you CAN'T," etc. And it will be some time before he will be able to stop. Remove the impression by the suggestion: "All right—all right."

THE "DRAWING" TEST.

Your next test may be that of *drawing him forward or backward toward you.* This is accomplished by standing before, or behind him, as the case may be, and telling him that he WILL walk toward you, backward or forward as you wish. The command must be made accompanied by the WILL. Remove the impression.

Akin to the last are two tests as follows: (1) *Preventing him from stepping out at all;* and (2) *preventing him from stepping outside of an imaginary circle that you have drawn on the floor.* These tests are of course accompanied by the appropriate suggestions, and use of the Will. Remove the impression.

THE "CHAIR" TESTS.

Similar tests such as *preventing him from sitting down in a chair;* or *causing him to remain seated in a chair, unable to rise;* may be made in the same way. Remove the impression.

OTHER TESTS.

Another common test is that of giving the "*impressionable*" a cane, telling him to hold it fast, and then telling him sharply that he cannot throw it down, for it is "*sticking* to your *hands,*" etc. Remove the impression.

A similar test is *preventing him from lifting* a light

weight, a box, or a chair by your suggestions of "you CAN'T" accompanied by the use of your Will. Remove the impression.

THE "NAME" TEST.

Some experimenters try the test of preventing the *"impressionable"* from speaking his name by their "CAN'T" suggestions. A variation of this is making him say his name is "Tom Jones," or some other fictitious name, by the mere strong suggestion of "Tom Jones, it's *Tom Jones,* I say," following upon the sharp question, "What's your name?" Strange as it may appear this test is successful in many instances. Remove the impression.

THE "EYELID" TEST.

The test of *fastening the eyelids* is accomplished by having the *"impressionable"* fasten his eyelids tight together, keeping them in that position for a few moments, when the experimenter says: "Now you CAN'T open them—you CAN'T—try, but you CAN'T," etc., etc., as above described. Release the impression.

Stiffening the arm, or leg, is accomplished along the same general lines using the appropriate suggestions and Will. Remove the impression.

THE "CATALEPSY" TEST.

The "catalepsy feat" of the professional hypnotists is but an enlargement of the above muscular tests, and consists of producing a condition of rigidity all over the body of the subject. I do not advise conducting this test, for accidents have occurred in some cases, and there are other reasons why it is not advisable. I mention it here merely as a matter of scientific interest. Notwithstanding the claims of the hypnotists that this test is capable of being produced only when the subject is in the "deep stage of hypnosis" known as the "cataleptic stage," all psychologists know that it may be produced in the wide-awake condition, and is merely a "muscular test," having nothing whatever to do with the "sleep-condition."

ONE UNDERLYING PRINCIPLE.

You will see that one law governs all of these tests, and thousands of others of a similar nature which may occur to the experimenter. It is all a matter of the use of the WILL and the SUGGESTION of the experimenter accompanied by the relaxation of the Will of the other person. The Law of Mentative Induction is the real cause behind the phenomena. The Suggestions render doubly efficient the Will Power of the experimenter, by giving the mind of the "*impressionable*" a mental image around which his Mental Poles materialize an action.

MUSCULAR TESTS, AND BEYOND.

The above tests are what are known as Muscular Tests, all depending upon the control of the muscles of the "*impressionable,*" by the Will of the experimenter. Many of these tests are believed by the Hypnotists and Mesmerists to be possible of production only when their "subjects" are in the "sleep condition," or at least only after they have been "put to sleep" and then aroused. As a matter of fact, sleep-conditions have nothing whatever to do with this phenomena, as may be proven by the fact that all of the above tests may be performed without any suggestion of sleep or similar condition.

There is a more remarkable class of phenomena than the above mentioned which will be considered in the next chapter, all of which, also, may be produced without any attempt to induce sleep. This sleep delusion has led people astray for many years, but now it is known that the phenomena of sleep itself is merely an *effect* of Mental Impression and Suggestion, instead of being the *cause* of the various phenomena known as Mesmerism and Hypnotism.

REMOVING THE IMPRESSION.

Referring to my repeated caution to "Remove the impression," I wish to call your attention to the fact that the best experimenters lay much stress upon the advisability, if not the absolute necessity, of *removing the induced condition* from the mind of the person experimented upon. Otherwise he might carry away with him the induced condition, or impression, which is often far deeper and stronger than is commonly believed to be the case. I URGE THIS UPON YOU specially. DO NOT NEGLECT IT. The conditions may readily be removed by the suggestion of "Now you are all right—all right now, you understand—you are NOW ALL RIGHT," accompanying the suggestion by the mental picture of their being relieved from the induced condition. The gentle touch of the hand, as in "patting" the part that has been controlled, will help to accentuate the effect of the suggestion of "all right."

REMOVING UNDESIRABLE CONDITIONS.

In this connection it may be as well to mention that if you ever happen to come across an "*impressionable*" with a tendency to manifest a drowsy condition, or the so-called "sleep-state" of hypnotism (probably arising from previous suggestions, either direct from a hypnotist or from having witnessed a hypnotic exhibition), you may proceed to awaken him in a similar way to the method just given for "Removing the Impression." In such case you may make upward passes along the sides of his head, saying to him sharply and positively, "WAKE UP—wake up now, I say—WAKE UP! WIDE AWAKE NOW—you're Wide Awake—wide awake! All right, now—ALL RIGHT, I say—ALL RIGHT! ALL RIGHT, and WIDE AWAKE! All Right—ALL RIGHT!" You may heighten the effect by snapping your fingers close to his face, and slapping his shoulders sharply. Be sure to speak positively, firmly and *sharply*, just as a father would in rousing up a sleepy boy in the morning, *and don't lose your head.*

You are not likely to have need for this advice, in ordinary experiments, but I give it in case you happen to come across some "*impressionable*" or "*hyper-impressionable*" (see later chapters) who may have been previously hypnotized by some operator who believed in the "sleep-condition," and brought same about by suggestion (see later chapters); or else some subject of the same class who has seen hypnotic subjects "go asleep," and induced the same state in himself by imitative self-impression. In such a case, I would advise that you afterward give the subject a good, sound suggestive treatment, to the effect that he will never again "go to sleep" in this way—that he is immune to hypnotic sleep suggestions—and in other ways build up in him a resistance to this deplorable condition. These "sleep-condition" hypnotists have much to answer for, for which their plea of ignorance is not quite sufficient.

CHAPTER IX.

EXPERIMENTS IN INDUCED SENSATION.

In the last chapter we considered instances of tests of Experimental Fascination, along the lines of Muscular Control. In this chapter we will consider the phenomena attendant upon Induced Sensation, all of which follows the same law of Cause, and is produced in the same manner, and by the same methods as the muscular phenomena.

Let us begin our consideration of Sense Control by the familiar test of the "Burning Hand."

THE "BURNING HAND" TEST.

This test is performed in the following manner: You stand before the "*impressionable,*" the latter extending his hand toward you palm downward. You place the first two fingers of your right hand upon the back of his hand, holding them there for a moment, and concentrating your gaze and Will upon his hand. Then you say to him, sharply, rapidly and positively: "I am burning your hand—I am burning your hand. It is *hot, hot, hot*—it is burning, burning, *burning you*—burning you *I say*—take it away, *quick,*

I tell you, it is *burning you,"* etc., etc. (always emphasizing the words "*hot*" and "*burning*") and at the same time Willing that your fingers will feel hot to him. It is surprising how many people will experience the sensation of heat, if you perform the test properly, and are able to concentrate your Will sufficiently well, and accompany the same with vivid suggestions. A variation of this test, is to give the "*impressionable*" a silver coin, telling him to hold it between his thumb and forefinger. Then after a moment give him the suggestions of it being "hot, *hot,* HOT—it's *burning* you, *burning you,"* etc. You may even impress upon him the idea that while it is burning him, he is unable to let go of it, etc.

INDUCED PAIN.

Another test of the sense of feeling is that shown by having the "*impressionable*" hold out his hand, his arm being extended full length. Then standing before him, with a pin between the finger and thumb of your right hand, pretend to prick *your own hand,* jabbing the pin into it, and grimacing as if with pain, at the same time saying to him: "You see, *you feel the pain* of this pin—it hurts you, *it hurts you, I say*—you feel the pain instead of my feeling it—*see,* you feel it *now* (making a feint of "jabbing" the pin into your own hand)—you *feel* it, I say, etc. It is remarkable how many persons will "take on" the pain that you are supposed to be feeling. Of course your imagination should be exercised, under the control of your Will, so that you will allow yourself to imagine that you feel the pain.

I have seen the above experiment tried before a room full of people, and many of the audience shared the induced pain with the *"impressionable"* upon whom the experiment was being tried. Do not forget what I said in the last chapter about taking away the induced condition after the test. In the above cases rub your finger over the burnt (?) or hurt (?) spot, saying: "It's all right now—*all right*—the pain is all gone." If you do not do so, the *"impressionable"* may carry away with him a sensation that his hand had been subjected to heat or pain.

REMARKABLE PHENOMENA.

In this connection, it may be proper to call your attention to the fact that the history of the subject shows cases in which burns have actually been produced on the bodies of persons by strong suggestions, coupled with physical aids, for instance, postage stamps have been placed on portions of the body, with the suggestion that they were fly-blisters, and the blister appeared. You will see that it is all a matter of "induced feeling," the more marked results merely evidencing the power of the mind of the individual over the mind in the portions of his body, as I have shown in the chapter entitled "Mental Therapeutics" in my work on "Mental Magic."

Many other experiments along the line of Sense Control, might be mentioned, but they are all but different forms of the same thing. The ingenuity of the experimenter will indicate manifold variations, if he sees fit to follow up the subject.

INDUCED SENSE OF SMELL.

The sense of Smell may be induced by the experimenter suggesting to the "*impressionable*" that a bottle contains a liquid smelling like certain perfumes, etc. This may be varied by changing the suggestion so that all the well-known perfumes may be sensed, like the legend of the magic perfume bottle of the wizard, which probably was nothing more than a case of clever induction of the sense of smell by the method mentioned herein.

PERSONAL EXPERIENCES.

I have seen a number of cases of this kind in my personal experience, in which large numbers of people were impressed in this way. In one case, I was attending a play, the scene of which was laid in the south, and in which one of the characters remarked "Oh, smell the magnolias—how strong is their odor in this heavy, warm night air," and in a moment the audience noticed a plain odor of magnolias floating over the house. So strong was the impression that many insisted that the management had actually introduced the odor, in order to heighten the effect, but inquiry showed this to be erroneous, for no odor was actually used.

More recently, I attended a play ("The Girl with the Green Eyes") in which one of the characters was supposed to have committed suicide by turning on the gas, in full sight of the audience. The room was large, and jet after jet of the many chandeliers, bracket-lights, etc., were turned on by the woman. In a short time people in the audience began to sniff, and say "Smell the gas," until everyone thought they smelled it, and some women felt faint. Of course, the original impression was given by the physical suggestion, but as soon as people took on the impression, it spread like a contagion, by the law of mental induction, until all felt it more or less.

THE PROFESSOR'S EXPERIMENT.

There are cases recorded of the effect being deliberately produced, for instance, the tale of the old German professor, who after telling his class that he would uncork a bottle containing a chemical compound noted for its foul odor, uncorked a bottle of distilled water, possessing no odor at all. The class soon perceived the supposed odor, and row after row of students showed their disgust. The waves of the supposed vapor floated over the room, just as would have been the case if the genuine liquid had been uncorked, those nearest the platform perceiving it first, and then the next row, and so on until the whole room was filled with it. Even after the professor explained the nature of the experiment, the class still sniffed away, and many refused to believe the explanation, so strong was the impression. These cases were nothing else than instances of induced sensation of smell, along the lines of Mental Impression.

INDUCED SIGHT.

The sense of Sight may be induced in the same way. A common experiment with a very impressionable person is as follows: tell him to extend his hand, palm down; then mark a cross on the back of his hand with your forefinger, pressing well into the skin, at the same time saying: "See, I have marked *a black cross* on your hand—*on your hand,* a black cross—*see it there*—you see it there now—black—*black—a black cross*—you see it there, don't you?" etc., and if he be sufficiently impressionable he will see it. The more that *you* can imagine the black cross there, the stronger will be *his* impression of it.

If you will call the attention of people to the extraordinary blueness of the sky, they will be very apt to acquiesce, some of them going into raptures over it, although the sky is no bluer than at any other time.

It is astonishing how many of these impressions are given and taken in every day life. Some one thinks the room is very close, and immediately many people begin to feel suffocated, and wish the windows raised. Someone suggests a draft, and people begin to shiver. Some one remarks how extremely warm the day is, and people begin to mop their foreheads. And so on —all being bits from the same piece.

INDUCED HEARING.

The sense of Hearing may be induced in the same way. Tell your *"impressionable"* that he hears the song of a bird, or the whistle of a locomotive, at the same time *using your own imagination* vigorously, and giving the suggestions sufficiently vividly, and he will hear the sounds mentioned. You may try this on several people in a room, on an ordinary occasion, by pretending to hear the humming of a bee, or a distant whistle, or some other faint sound such as the distant wail of a child, and a certain percentage of those present, after a moment or two of intent listening, will affirm that they heard the sound.

INDUCED TASTE.

The sense of taste is easily induced. The well known experiment of suggesting the taste of lemons, with the accompaning flow of saliva and taste of acid, is a good example. With a good *"impressionable"* you may induce a sense of changing tastes from extreme sweetness to extreme acidity, in a simple tasteless glass of water—it all depends upon the degree of impressionability of the persons tested, and the strength of your own imagination and suggestion. It is all a question of induced sensation. The professional hypnotist turns this to good account in his entertainment.

PERSONAL EXPERIMENTS.

In this connection I would say that several years ago when I was devoting much time to experimental work, I cured many cases of tobacco-chewing, cigarette habit, etc., by a course of vivid suggestion, accompanied by visualization, manifesting as mental induction. I would create a mental image of the tobacco or cigarettes as having a disgusting taste,—a taste that produced a feeling akin to nausea—and then would concentrate my mind and feeling upon the other person, giving him at the same time the most vivid suggestions of "disgusting, nauseating, sickening taste," etc., etc., etc., until he would be unable to chew the tobacco, or smoke the cigarette. Then by following up the matter by giving him the strongest "future impression" that he would always remember the sensation of disgusting taste whenever he attempted to chew or smoke, and that the tobacco or cigarette would always induce those feelings in him, a cure of the habit would be effected.

"SLEEP-CONDITION" NOT NECESSARY.

Some practitioners of Suggestive Therapeutics have met with much success in the treatment of undesirable habits in this way. It is true that many of these practitioners have believed that it was necessary to produce the "hypnotic sleep" in order to get the results, but this is simply because they themselves are "self-hypnotized" with the "sleep-delusion," and if they would but throw off their spell, and begin to experiment along the other lines, they would see that the same results could be obtained without the slightest attempt to produce sleep.

SENSES INHIBITED.

Just as the senses may be rendered by induction, so may they be inhibited in the same way. Any of the above experiments with the senses may be reversed at Will. Tell your *"impressionable"* that he *cannot* hear a certain sound; smell a certain odor; taste a certain taste; feel a certain sensation; see a certain thing; and if you be sufficiently Positive, and he sufficiently impressionable, and if you use your imagination and suggestion sufficiently well—the senses will be inhibited in his mind for the time being.

REMARKABLE INSTANCES.

In the matter of inhibition of the sense of Feeling, some most remarkable results may be obtained—in fact all of the results along this line secured by the hypnotists with the aid of the "deep-sleep," may be obtained without attempt at sleep. I have seen minor operations performed under the influence of induced inhibition of the sense of feeling. I have seen teeth extracted with little or no pain in this way. I have seen nervous patients, unusually sensitive to pain, able to stand dental work with practically no discomfort, by means of such inhibition of the sense of feeling. Even the brutal experiments of many of the stage hypnotists, who run needles through hypnotized patient's cheeks, without causing pain—even these can be duplicated without sleep being induced, although I consider such exhibitions deplorable and disgusting, and worthy of the severest condemnation. I merely mention these last to show the power of induced feeling, or inhibition of the same by induction.

THE SECRET OF INHIBITION.

The secret of the inhibition of the senses, is that the Will is directed to "shutting off" the attention to the part or organ. If the Attention can be removed, or shut off, no pain will be felt. Many persons have practiced on themselves, until they can inhibit pain in portions of their body. And in inducing the effect in another person, the same methods are used, accompanied by suggestion.

MENTAL ANÆSTHESIA.

It may be of interest to many students, to have me make a little more detailed reference to this subject of Anæsthesia by Mental Induction. Anæsthesia, you know is "an entire or partial loss or absence of feeling or sensation." We generally think of this condition as being brought about only by something like ether, gas, etc. But anything that will tend to inhibit sensation is an "anæsthetic." The word "inhibit," you know, means "to check; to hold back; to restrain," etc. And pain and sensation may be inhibited by pure Mental Impression.

HISTORICAL INSTANCES.

History is full of instances of inhibition of pain, by strong mental feeling, emotion, ecstasy, etc. Religious fanatics have mutilated themselves barbarously, without feeling the pain. The American Indians in their wild dances, wound themselves without feeling the pain. In India the fanatical devotees torture themselves in horrible ways, as a religious rite, and seem entirely callous to pain. People have been burned at the stake, chanting joyful songs, and martyrs have been crunched in the jaws of the wild beasts with laughter and joy fully manifest. All of these instances, and many others of the same kind, show that it is possible for the mind of a person to inhibit pain in himself. And, the inhibition of pain in a person, by another person, is merely a calling into play of the same power, by means of induction and suggestion.

It is not a creation of the power in the person, but *merely a calling forth that which is already there.*

HOW TO INHIBIT PAIN IN ANOTHER.

The following simple, but very effective, method is that used in the best psychological laboratories. The "*impressionable*" is comfortably seated, or placed in a reclining position, before the experimenter. Let us suppose that it is wished to inhibit sensation in his arm. In that case the experimenter will begin to stroke the arm *upward,* from finger tips to shoulder. The effect of this stroking is to restrain the circulation, which latter responds readily to such suggestion, as we shall see a little later on. The experimenter says: "Now I am taking the circulation away from your arm, and putting the nerves to rest. You will begin to feel a sensation of *coolness* and *numbness* coming over your arm, from finger tips to shoulder. Now you feel it—your arm is getting numb, *numb,* I say—*quite numb.* Getting *numb*—getting *numb*—getting *numb—numb*—NUMB—NUMB. It is now *quite numb.* You cannot feel pain in it. See, I will prick it with this needle, but you *will not feel pain.* You can feel the *touch,* but cannot feel any *pain,*" and so on, until complete inhibition is effected. When you first prick with the point of the needle, do so but gently, although appearing to do it with force—this will reassure the patient, and will make him relax his resisting Will the more.

RESULT OF REPETITION.

The above process continued, in the right person, and in the proper manner, will produce wonderful results. In fact, in this way is the inhibition of sensation produced, in order that minor operations may be performed without the use of ether, etc. A little practice for several days, renders the effect more marked each time, until the desired degree is obtained. The above method is the most simple, and yet the most effective, known to experimental psychologists, and if persisted in, and performed intelligently, is capable of wonderful development. It should be unnecessary for me to add that the experimenter should keep before his own mind, vividly, the condition he wishes to produce in the patient. He should endeavor to actually "see" him insensible to pain, and should throw his whole belief and earnestness into the suggestions. More than "lip service" is necessary.

DIRECTING THE CIRCULATION.

In connection with the above experiments, the following is interesting. You may take an impressionable person, and increase the circulation in any part of the body, or else inhibit it partially, just as you wish. You may prove this by ordering the circulation back in one arm, and increasing it in another, the result being that one hand will be a ghastly white, and the other a deep red color. Blood may be drawn away from the head in this manner, and headaches thereby relieved. But, I must stop this, for I am encroaching upon the subject of Mental Therapeutics. In this direction of the circulation upward or downward (as the case may be) passes of the hands will prove of great assistance, for this motion is followed by the Attention, and an axiom in Suggestive Therapeutics is that "The Circulation follows the Attention." Downward passes increase the circulation to the limbs—upward ones inhibit it.

I have spoken of the above effects being produced upon the "*impressionables.*" I mean by this, that such people are the more readily affected. But, remember this, that even the strongest willed man or woman may be affected in this manner, if he or she will by directing this Will, actually *co-operate* in the matter. For instance, the very strength of a man's Will may aid in the inhibition of pain by Suggestion, because he will be *co-operating with the Suggestor.* All the effect comes from "the power within" in any case—and all the experimenter or suggestor does is *to call that power into effect.* It is akin to driving a team of strong horses, or the running of a 1,000 horsepower engine—the power is not in the driver or engineer, *but they make the thing go, nevertheless.*

In closing this chapter, let me again impress upon the experimenter the importance of *always removing the impression* after the experiment. Remember the important final "Now you're *all right—all right now—all right!*"

In the next chapter we pass on to the consideration of the Phenomena of Induced Imagination.

CHAPTER X.

THE PHENOMENA OF INDUCED IMAGINATION.

I will now lead you to a consideration of a class of experiments more marked in sensational features than those related in the previous two chapters. These experiments are the ones usually alluded to as "the higher hypnotic phenomena," although they really are as distinct from the "hypnotic" or sleep condition, as the ones already considered. Any and all forms of the "hypnotic" phenomena, may be produced without resorting to the methods of the hypnotists so far as producing the sleep condition is concerned. I call this class of phenomena "Induced Imagination."

WHAT IMAGINATION IS.

The term "Imagination," you know, means "The power of the mind to create mental images of objects of sense; the power to reconstruct or recombine the materials furnished by experience, memory or fancy; a mental image formed by the faculty of imagination," etc., etc. The word is derived from the English word "Image," which in turn has for its root the Latin word "*imatari,*" meaning "to imitate."

IMAGINATION AND FANCY.

The Imagination is creative in its nature and works with the plastic material of the mind. The writers usually make a distinction between what is called "imagination proper," on the one hand, and what is called "fancy" on the other. By "imagination proper" is meant the higher forms of activity of the image-creating faculty, such as is manifested in the creation of literature, art, music, philosophical theory, scientific hypothesis, etc. By "fancy" is meant the lighter forms of the manifestation of the image-creating faculty, such as the ideal fancies and day-dreams of people; the arbitrary and capricious imaginings; fantasy, etc. "Imagination proper" may be considered as a Positive phase, and "Fancy" as the Negative phase, of the Image-creating faculty.

POSITIVE IMAGINATION.

Imagination in its Positive phase is a most important faculty of the human being. It lies at the basis of active mental manifestation. One must form a mental image of a thing before he can manifest it in objective form. It is distinctly creative in its nature, and really forms the mould in which deeds and actions are cast—it forms the architect's plan, which we use to build our life of action and deeds. And, *mind you this,* it is the faculty used in the Occult practice known as "Visualization," which is spoken of in my work on "Mental Magic." Positive Imagination is very far from being the fanciful, capricious, light, whimsical thing that many suppose it to be. It is one of the most positive manifestations of the mind. Not only does it precede, and is necessary to, the performance of objective acts, and the producing of material things—but it is also the faculty by which we impress our mental-images upon the minds of others by Mentative Induction, and by the use of Desire and Will. Positive Imagination is the mother of "Ideas." And "idea" is but "an image formed in the mind" (Webster), and the Imagination is the faculty in which the "image" (or "idea") is formed. And in proportion to the activity of the Imagination, so is the strength of the image or idea. And as is the strength of the image or idea, so is the degree of its power to impress itself upon the minds of others. So you see, Imagination, in its Positive phase is a strong, real thing. But it is largely with its Negative phase that we shall have to deal with here.

THE NATURE OF MESMERIC CONTROL.

All of you who have witnessed an exhibition of mesmerism, or hypnotism, or else read descriptions of the same, have doubtless marveled at the phenomenon of the "subject" performing all sorts of ridiculous and peculiar actions under the direction of the hypnotist. There have been many theories advanced to account for this phenomenon, some of them very complicated and labored. But I have discarded theory after theory of this kind, finding them inadequate to explain the mental processes involved, much less the underlying principle. I have come to a conclusion arising from my own investigation and experiments, which I shall give you here. This "theory"—or explanation, for it is scarcely a "theory"—does not attempt to go into the "what is mind" question, nor does it attempt to divide or sub-divide the mind. It merely explains the "workings of the mind" in this class of phenomena.

AN EXPLANATION.

The explanation just mentioned is as follows: I hold that the action of the "hypnotic subject" may be explained upon the hypothesis that his "Negative Imagination," or Fancy, if you prefer to call it such, is acted upon by the Suggestions and Mentative Currents of the operator, and an induced state of Negative Imagination is set up. That is to say that, in hypnotic phenomena, instead of the subject's Negative Imagination being aroused by his own Desire or Will, or other planes of his Mentality, such condition is aroused by Mentative Induction, caused by the Mentative Currents of the operator, and aided by Suggestion. Let us see whether this is reasonable.

INDUCED IMAGINATION.

All of you know that your Negative Imagination may be aroused by outward persons or things. You hear a piece of music, and before you know it your Fancy is running along painting all sorts of pictures in your mind, and inducing all sorts of feelings. A picture may affect you in the same way. A piece of poetry, or poem, may lift you out of yourself on the wings of Fancy. A book may carry you along in a world of fantasy and unreality, until you forget the actual world around you—have you not had this experience? And, more marked than any of the above mentioned cases, is the effect of a perfect stage performance, in which the world and characters of the play take such a hold upon you as to seem reality itself, and you laugh and cry with the characters in the play. You scowl at the villain, and tremble at the danger of the heroine. You glory in the hero's success, and shed tears at the sorrows and trials of the suffering characters. And you feel these things in proportion that your Negative Imagination or Fancy is called into activity by induction. But remember this—the actors, poet, writer, composer, or artist *created* his effect by the exercise of his or her *Positive* Imagination; while the effect upon you is induced in your Negative

Imagination. The first is an act of Positive Creation, while the second is merely a *Reflection* impressed upon your mind, by either the Suggestion, or the Mentative Energy of the actor.

In your consideration of the above, remember what I have said about Suggestion, in an earlier chapter. Suggestion is merely the presentation of the Outward Symbol of the Inner Feeling.

THE MISTAKE OF THE SUGGESTIONISTS.

The radical school of Suggestionists pooh-pooh at the idea of Mentative Energy having anything to do with the phenomena which we are now considering. They claim that "Suggestion" is sufficient to account for it all. Without going deeply into a discussion of this matter, I would ask these gentlemen: *Why is it that the same words, uttered in the same tone, by two different suggestors, produce widely different degrees of effect?* Also: What is that peculiar Personal Force that we FEEL when certain persons Suggest, that is absent in the Suggestions of others? My answer is that the difference lies in the degree of Feeling called into activity in the mind of the Suggestor—*the degree of Mentative Energy released by him.* And I think that any careful investigator will agree with me in this, if he will open his mind to all the impressions received during his investigations, instead of tying himself to a previously conceived theory.

HIGHLY IMPRESSIONABLE SUBJECT.

Now here is an important feature of this matter of the phenomena which we are considering. The investigator will find that while the conditions mentioned in the two last chapters—the muscular and sense induction, respectively, may be produced in a large percentage of the *"impressionables,"* still there are comparatively few of them in which the more startling phases may be induced. Why is this? The answer is that there are a certain number of persons who combine within themselves the negative qualities of the *"impressionables,"* combined with a highly developed faculty of Fancy, or Negative Imagination. This combination causes the person possessing it to be an ideal subject for these strange experiments referred to. Such a person is what the French hypnotists call a *"somnambule,"* or hyper-sensitive, but which terms I discard because of their hypnotic association, and I substitute the term *"hyper-impressionables."* I have explained the sense in which I use the term *"impressionable."* The word *"hyper"* is a prefix, meaning "over; above; excessive; abnormally great," etc. The term *"hyper-impressionables,"* as I shall use it, means an "abnormally impressionable" person. This excessive, or abnormally great, impressionability, as I have said, arises from *the combination of a Negative Will with an excessive faculty of Fancy,* the latter being a form of Negative Imagination, remember. So you see that the taint of negativity is all over these persons.

A PSYCHOLOGICAL COMBINATION.

In order to show that I am correct in this classification, I will call your attention to the fact that an ordinary *"impressionable,"* even though his Will-Power be the weakest, cannot be induced to perform the tests of the *"hyper-impressionable"* if his faculty of Fancy be not excessive. And on the other hand, one may take a person of highly developed Positive Imagination—and our great people in all lines are such—and they are most difficult to influence in this way. In fact they are constantly affecting and influencing others. The strongest influencers of men belong to this last mentioned class. So you see the ideal *"hyper-impressionable"* must have the combination of Negativity, and Fancy. He is in a class all by himself. Let us examine him.

THE "HYPER-IMPRESSIONABLE."

In the first place, he is most credulous, superstitious, fanciful, bigoted, and unstable. He is of the class whose fancy is easily aroused, and induced, and whose general tendency is toward "giving airy nothings a local habitation and a name," and to whom "when shown an egg, the next minute the air is full of feathers." He is also prone to Imitation, and is inclined to "follow my leader," rather than to strike out a new path for himself. He has but little Originality and Initiative, which are highly developed in the man of strong Positive Imagination. He resembles the sheep and goose, rather than the eagle or lion. He is always dependent upon others for ideas, information, advice, and often material support. His Imagination is negative, that is, has little or no *original action,* and acts only (and easily) when induced or excited by another's mentality or suggestion. He has no executive ability, and feels easier when he has someone to "order him around," and to tell him what to do. He is a good copyer, mimic, and imitator, and is often quite serviceable in positions where the work is mechanical and a "good copyer" is needed.

The mysterious and unusual has a fascination for him akin to the fascination exerted over some birds by a waving bit of colored cloth. He is governed by his emotions rather than by his reason. He is excessively fanciful and "imaginative" (as the term is generally used) and has a decidedly hysterical tendency, and a disposition to "see things" and to "feel strangely"—he has many "strange experiences." He has but a minimum of self-control, and is apt to "fly-off" readily. He lacks voluntary attention, and application, and his mind is apt to "go a-wandering"—the only time that he can be kept steady is when some Positive Individual controls and superintends him. The excitable, emotional colored man, who gets religion at every camp-meeting, only to backslide next week, is an illustration of one class of this type. He "takes-on" the mental states of those around him, readily, and accepts readily a strong, positive suggestion. These are some of his characteristics.

THE "EAR-MARKS."

There are many of these people in the world, in high and low life. But, high or low, there is a strong family resemblance in their mental make-up. The two great characteristics by which they may be distinguished are, as stated, (1) A NEGATIVE WILL, and (2) an excessive faculty of Fancy. These two combine to manifest a highly marked example of NEGATIVE IMAGINATION.

THE "PRIZE-SUBJECTS" OF THE HYPNOTISTS.

Now, the reason that I have gone into the matter of the nature and character of the "*hyper-impressionable*" people is this: *It is from the ranks of these people that the "subjects" of the hypnotists are recruited. If you understand the nature of these people, you will understand how the phenomena are produced.* Of course the majority of professional hypnotists deny this, and make great claims that their "subjects" belong to a class of people having peculiar qualities owing to ability to concentrate, etc., but every one of them knows in his heart that my above statement is true. Those who have had the opportunity of personal acquaintance with these "subjects" know that they all come under the above classification, with the exception of those persons known as "horses," the name which the professional hypnotists give to people who travel around as "professional subjects" and who play their parts just as any other actor does. These "horses" are trained to go through their parts and also to serve as "bell-wethers" or leaders of the flock of "*hyper-impressionables*" who are taken from the audience. I know just what I am talking about when I make this statement, notwithstanding the commonly accepted opinion of the uninformed public to the effect that the prize subjects are just the average run of folks. Now let us attend an imaginary public hypnotic performance, in order to form a clear understanding of the matter.

CHAPTER XI.

AN INQUIRY INTO CERTAIN PHENOMENA.

And now for our public hypnotic performance. Take your seats, please.

THE HYPNOTIC PERFORMANCE.

The audience is seated, and the hypnotist appears. He makes a nice little introductory speech, in which he gives the history of hypnotism and mesmerism. He avoids the scientific side of the subject, except such parts of it as serve to arouse the interest of the audience. He points out to the audience that the commonly accepted opinion of the subjects being "weak-willed," etc., is erroneous, and that so far from this being the fact, no one except persons having will-power and the ability to concentrate may be hypnotized. He mentions the time-worn tale that idiots and insane people, and very young children, are not amenable to hypnotic influence, and from these things he draws the moral that the ability to be hypnotized is an honor and a proof of one's strong mentality, rather than otherwise. This, of course, flatters the "*hyper-impressionables,*" who always flock to a public hypnotic performance, being drawn there by their love of the curious, and *the fascination that such exhibitions seem to have for these people.*

THE CALL FOR SUBJECTS.

The hypnotist then calls for volunteer subjects. The audience does not seem to be in a hurry to respond, although some are found to be fidgeting in their chairs, and a few almost rise from their seats as if to go forward. The hypnotist encourages, and commands, "Come on, come on, now; right up this way; come right up," etc., and the inclination to "come forward" grows stronger. Then a young man starts forward with a rush, and then another from the other side of the house. Then maybe a third or a fourth—and then comes the grand rush. These first people to move forward are usually the paid performers who travel with the hypnotist, and their coming to the front starts up the "*impressionables*" and "*hyper-impressionables*" among the audience, and perhaps a few curiosity seekers. These paid performers act as "bell-wethers" for the flock of human sheep.

TESTING AND SELECTING SUBJECTS.

The volunteer subjects (including the paid ones) are now grouped around the back of the stage in a large semi-circle. And then the hypnotist proceeds to "test" them. He usually starts off by bidding the semi-circle gaze at their hands, or upon some bright object placed in their fingers. After they have quieted down and have been rendered passive and attentive, he calls them one by one to the front and gives them a test for impressionability. He usually begins with the paid subjects, for he knows just what they will do. and their actions have a powerful impression on the others along the lines of imitative suggestion. He usually tries the "falling backward and forward test," and perhaps the "fastening of the hands," or some other simple muscular test. Those who respond readily to these tests are accepted and instructed to sit down again, while those who fail to respond are told that they are not needed, and resume their places in the audience. The hypnotist must have reasonably "sure things" to work upon for his success upon producing a quick result, and he cannot afford to devote the time to "developing" subjects that the experimenter in the laboratory does. Finally he has weeded the goats from the sheep, the former being retired to the audience and the latter exalted to places of honor on the stage, having successfully passed their initiation and now being "accepted subjects."

THE STORY OF THE "PAID SUBJECTS."

Now, just a moment here about the "paid subjects." Some of them are genuine "*hyper-impressionables,*" who are fascinated by the mysterious nature of "the business" and flattered by the position of prominence given them in the performance, and who travel around with the hypnotist on a small salary and board paid. The "horses" are different kind of people—they are "out for the money" alone, and are generally "fakirs" all the way through. They have trained themselves to stand pain and to allow needles to be thrust through their cheeks and similar rough treatment to be accorded them. They learn to act out their parts with a surprising degree of ability in some cases, and many of them in time graduate into the cheaper grade of variety actors, and a few mount even higher up and develop genuine talent as actors. The majority of them, however, belong to the "cigarette type" of youth, who "is out for a good time" and who is glad to play his part in the performance for his board, traveling expenses, cigarette money, a little loose change, and the cheap notoriety of public performance. Some of the more expert of them demand and receive larger salaries as they advance in the scale, and a few "star performers" in the business receive quite good salaries—and earn it, too. These "horses" often display considerable ability in the line of suggestion and really lead the volunteer subjects through their acts, the latter obeying the line of least resistance along the general lines of imitative suggestion. These "star performers" among the "horses" are often just as expert hypnotists as their employers, and consequently much of the success of the "entertainment" is due to their efforts.

PRODUCING "SLEEP" (?).

The next stage in the performance is to induce "sleep" (?) in the subjects. This is done by first inducing fixation of the eye-lids, along the lines of muscular control of which I have spoken. Then suggestions of sleep are given by the hypnotist, such as "You are growing drowsy, drowsy, drowsy—your eyelids are heavy, heavy, heavy as lead—you are falling asleep, falling asleep," etc., and soon the heads of the "horses" and the "*hyper-impressionables*" are nodding. The "*impressionables*" who are not affected by the sleep suggestions are sorted out and sent back to the audience, until there is left only the "horses" and "*hyper-impressionables,*" including the paid performers among the latter, as well as those who have volunteered. Then the hypnotist has obtained that which he has tried for. He has a circle of "*hyper-impressionables*" and "horses" who will accept every suggestion that he may give them, and be responsive to every demand upon their Negative Imagination that he may induce in them.

THE "DAY-DREAM" CONDITION.

"But are they not really asleep?" you may ask. No! they are not asleep. Their condition is one of a drowsy, day-dreamy state, such as many of us have felt when lost in reverie, or "absent-mindedness." They have had the feeling of "drowsiness" induced in them by the suggestions and influence of the hypnotist and have had their Negative Imagination acted upon by him until they are in a state of dazed day-dream. They know what is going on about them and realize the illusion which they are acting out, but are so passive that their imagination is partially beyond their own control and is induced and managed by the hypnotist through his Positive Imagination and his Suggestions. It is a queer state. I have talked with many of these people and think that I have measured the mental state existing in them. They are living in two worlds. Their Wills are passive—and the Negative Imagination, or Fancy, is most active and under the control of the hypnotist.

THE "PLAYING-BEAR" EXPLANATION.

An illustration that I have used in some of my lectures on this subject may give you a clearer idea of the matter. It is as follows: A party of children are playing "bear." One of them is the bear and goes growling, wagging his head, and showing his teeth in a ferocious manner. The other children pretend to be frightened, but after a bit they induce in themselves a feeling of real terror—the assumed becomes almost real to them. (Children have very vivid Negative Imaginations and often suffer great torture by foolish suggestions of "boogy-man;" "big bear catch you;" "something will grab you when you go upstairs," etc. An understanding of suggestion would show the folly and criminality of such things.) The terror among the children grows more acute, and tears mingle with laughter as they run from the "bear." At last one of the youngest runs with a shriek to its mother and buries its little face in her lap, crying out, "Make him go 'way." "Why, that isn't a bear, Mary—that's only Johnny dressed up like one," says the mother, endeavoring to quiet the little one. "Yes, I know it is," sobs little Mary, venturing a frightened glance behind her; "but I'm scared, anyhow." Well, that is the condition of the "*hyper-impressionable*" who is hypnotized. *He "knows it's only Johnny, but he is scared anyhow!"* It is not all a make-believe, as some radical iconoclastic investigators have affirmed—it's half real and half unreal. The hypnotized "*hyper-impressionable*" is not a "fakir" or a wilful deceiver—he is a "make-believe," whose illusion seems half real, or even more so, although less than half in some cases, the degree of reality varying with the degree of impressionability on the one hand and the vividness of the Negative Imagination on the other.

OPPOSING VIEWS RECONCILED.

I have gone into this matter of the mental state of the genuine hypnotic subject rather fully, for the reason that the statements of two schools of investigators are diametrically opposed to each other on the subject. The old school of mesmerists and hypnotists insists that the subjects are in a "true-sleep" condition, and are absolutely oblivious to all that goes on around them, outside of their illusions—that they are acting out dreams suggested to them. The new school of "Suggestion," on the other hand, claims that the subjects are wide-awake as usual and merely acquiesce in the suggestions made them, just as they would in any other, and are fully conscious of what they are doing, and are "make-believe" all the way through, from beginning to end. I think that my theory, or explanation, will supply the Reconciliation, or Missing-link, between these two opposing views, and I believe that it will meet with the approval of many who, like myself, have had the opportunity of examining these people and getting close to the heart of the matter. It is true that many of these subjects will tell you that they were totally unconscious of what they were doing, but that is because in so doing they are carrying out the suggestions, express or implied, of the hypnotist, who tells them that they are 'hypnotized" and know nothing else. A funny thing about these subjects is that each one of them thinks that he is the only one who was "half-awake," and that all of his companions were "completely under" the influence. Remember, now, I am not talking of "trance conditions," which belong to another phase of the subject, nor am I talking about the "horses" on the stage, who are "fakirs" all the way through, although contributing much to the interest and action of the show. My description of the mental state of the subject applies only to the genuine cases of hyper-impressionability, in the "day-dream" state.

THE HYPNOTIC SHOW.

I shall not take up your time and space by describing the many features of the public hypnotic performance—the barber-shop scene; the balloon trip; the baseball game; the hive of bees; the school session; and the thousand of variations shown by the many hypnotic exhibitors and performers, some of whom are artists in their line, and show a wonderful ability in the direction of making their performances "interesting" and akin to a vaudeville show. Nearly everyone who reads these lines has seen a performance of this sort and will know to what I refer. The principle is the same in all of these acts or performances. The "horses" and the "*hyper-impressionables*" accept the suggestions, and the latter are also impressed by the hypnotist's Positive Imagination acting upon their Negative Imagination through Mental Currents by Induction.

But even the most startling and complicated experiments are but combinations of the experiments in "Induced Sensation" mentioned in Chapter IX of this book, raised to a superlative degree by means of "Induced Imagination." The experiments I have given you, and others of the same kind, are the building-blocks from which the mesmeric structures are built,—the style, variety, decoration, and stability, depending upon the art of the operator or manager. There are many books on Stage Hypnotism that instruct the performer in constructing "effective scenes." It is a matter of stage art, rather than of scientific knowledge.

The successful hypnotist must be a man of strong suggestive ability—one able to focus his force in his tones, and also of strong, active Positive Imagination, and thus able to form a clear, vivid Mental Picture of the scene he wishes to be enacted on the stage before him. By forming this Mental Picture and by using his Will to project and focus his Mentative Energy upon the subjects he is able to induce in them the feelings and day-dreams desired. His success as an entertainer, of course, requires ability as an originator of scenes, etc., which have nothing whatever to do with his ability as a hypnotist. When both qualities are combined the man comes to the front as a financial success.

PRIVATE EXPERIMENTS, ETC.

While the above has dealt solely with public performances of hypnotism, still the principles called into play in the private psychological experimental work are the same. In the latter there is no audience to be entertained, and much more time may be devoted to "developing" a subject and producing interesting phenomena, and the "horses" are eliminated.

CHAPTER XII.

THE DANGERS OF PSYCHISM.

In the preceding chapters I have gone into the subject of the rationale of Mesmerism, for the purpose of pointing out to you that the phenomena of Mesmerism and Hypnotism is not dependent upon "sleep-conditions," but may be readily produced by Mental Fascination, pure and simple, without any attempt to bring about the "sleep" which is publicly associated with the phenomena. I have not only pointed out the general principles underlying the subject, but have given in detail the technique and methods whereby the phenomena may be produced by any experimenter. The methods given therein are the ones in constant use in the leading psychological experimental laboratories of this and other countries, and the results mentioned may be duplicated by any person who will put into operation the principles mentioned.

WHY THE INFORMATION IS IMPARTED.

But I wish to state that my primary object in imparting the said information was not that the students of the book must necessarily undertake a series of psychological experiments, but principally that they might understand the power and force of the mental principle known as "Mental Fascination," and see its practical operation in all of its varied phases. I wish them to know the experiments in the psychological laboratory; the "performances" of the public mesmerist, or hypnotist; and the use of Mental Influence in business and everyday life that we see in operation around us on all sides, and at all times, are all phases of the same underlying principle. I wish to show them the *oneness* in essence of all these varying phases of operation of this great mental principle.

CERTAIN PHASES MENTIONED.

There is one phase of mesmeric, or hypnotic, phenomena, however, that I have omitted. I shall call your attention to this briefly, that you may know that I have not overlooked the same, and also that you may recognize my reasons for not going into detail regarding this class of phenomena. I allude to the so-called "higher phases" of mesmeric or hypnotic phenomena—the various forms of the "trance condition."

THE ABNORMAL CONDITIONS.

This "trance" phenomena, whether produced by mesmeric processes or by other means, are abnormal, unhealthy, and undesirable phases of mental condition. I cannot speak too strongly against the encouragement of, and instruction in, the development (I had almost said the "Devil-opment") of these abnormal states, either by self-practice or by means of hypnotic or mesmeric practices. It is high time that someone should call the attention of the public to the dangers of this so-called "psychism." I *know positively* that this "psychism" is not the desirable thing that it is supposed to be. I know, also, that *it is very far from true Occult Development.* This "psychism," when compared with true Occultism, is but as the baleful glare of the Moon, as contrasted with the bright, warm, life-giving rays of the Sun. This false Occultism, which is not Occultism at all, but is merely "psychism," has deluded many into its folds, and has led its followers on to planes which are akin to mental quagmires and swamps, following the *ignis fatuus,* or will-o'-the-wisp" of "Psychism."

THE ANTIQUITY OF THE PRACTICES.

Nearly all races of men have discovered that there are means possible to people whereby they may produce in themselves abnormal conditions, known as the "trance." And men, from the dim past to the present time, have seen fit to indulge in these deplorable practices. The means by which these states are obtained are various, the favorite methods being the gazing at a bright object; fixing the gaze at the root of the nose; staring at the umbilicus; staring at a drop of ink; inhaling vapors; listening to wierd music, etc., etc. Much mock-occultism, which is really "psychism," depends upon these methods for its results, manifestation, and phenomena. The Hindu fakirs and the Arab dervishes indulge freely in these methods, and produce results which while highly esteemed by themselves, are viewed with disgust, horror and repulsion by true Occultists of all lands, including, of course, the *real* Hindu Yogis and Persian Sufis, both of which last mentioned bodies of Oriental Occultists regard these practices as harmful, and the phenomena resulting therefrom as bogus and misleading.

WESTERN FALLACIES.

And much of the latter-day Western Psychism is also based upon the same practices, and brings about like results. In this connection I would say that some of the practices adopted by some of the "New Thought" people belong to this class. I have seen methods advised for "Going into the Silence," in which the student is advised to focus his gaze on the root of his nose, etc., which is the identical method used by Braid to produce hypnotic conditions, and which is also used by the Hindu fakirs to produce "trance" conditions. Is it not time that the truth regarding these things should be known?

LOW STATES NOT HIGH CONDITIONS.

These self-induced abnormal conditions may also be produced by hypnotic methods, by leading the subject into the "deeper stages," which some authorities speak of as if they were "highly spiritual," but which are nothing more than the miserable, abnormal, deplorable 'trance" conditions just referred to. These conditions may be produced by hypnotic methods, simply because *any mental state may be so produced,* and not because of any mystic process, or knowledge, or connection. Let us take another hasty glance at the so-called "sleep-conditions" of hypnotism, that we may get a clear idea of the subject.

THE "SLEEP DELUSION."

In the first place, there is no *real* "sleep-condition." Let us see why this is. Well, to start from the beginning, much of the "sleep" does not exist at all. In some cases the subject merely acquiesces in the suggestion that he is asleep, and then he acts out the suggestion, just as he would act out *any* suggestion. He plays out his part—that's all. This phase is far more common than the majority of students of hypnotism are aware of. They hear the subject say that he was asleep, and did not remember a thing that was said to him, or what he did. But all of this is merely in the line of acquiescence, and "playing the part," which fact has been positively proven by advanced experimenters. But there are other stages of "sleep." The next in order is the "day-dream" stage, which I have described as the "playing-bear" phase. Even this is not a true sleep, but a condition resembling a day-dream. It is in this stage that the majority of instances of hypnotic phenomena are produced. Sometimes the "day-dream" becomes very deep, and the "trance" condition is almost reached. But still it is not "sleep" as the word is generally used.

HYPNOTIC TRANCES DEPLORED.

Next in order come the several stages of the condition which hypnotists speak of as "deep-sleep" conditions, but which I state positively are nothing more or less than the well known "trance" conditions into which people of all nations and times have plunged themselves by the methods before mentioned. The only difference is that the operator induces the condition by Mental Influence, and Suggestion, just as he would induce any other mental state—instead of the subject inducing it in himself. It is the same old abnormal, harmful practice, in another guise. And anything that is said against the self-induced condition is equally applicable to the operator-induced one. They are the same thing!

WILL-WEAKENING PRACTICES.

I shall not describe the conditions at further length, nor shall I give any instructions in the production of them. I consider them essentially harmful, and my object in speaking of them here is to warn off and caution anyone from allowing themselves to be placed in this condition by experimenters. The practice is weakening to the Will, for the reason that it depends upon the tiring out of the Will by straining the eyes or other organs of sense. Practitioners of Mental Influence in all ages have recognized this fact and have employed objects calculated to tire out the Will. Bright objects to stare at and thus tire out the sense of sight have been employed; monotonous sounds ending in "*um-m-m-m-m*" are used by the Orientals to tire out the sense of hearing by its monotonous and soothing sound; vapors and perfumes and incense are used to overcome the sense of smell—all tending to tire out the Will, and to reduce it to a Passive, non-resisting stage. Then when the Will has been rendered Passive, or tired, the mind becomes receptive and impressionable, and, in extreme cases, becomes as wax in the hands of the operator. Remember these things, students, and you will see this principle called into operation many times, in unexpected places. Beware of the methods that tend to drug the Will.

PSYCHISM LIKE A POISONOUS COBRA.

Let me urge upon you to avoid "Psychism"—put it away from you as you would a poisonous cobra, for it seeks to strike at the heart of your Will, and would thus paralyze your mentality. Beware of all that tends to make you Weak. Beware of the claims of "soul-development" or "spiritual-unfoldment" that are accompanied by these methods, for they are but Psychism masquerading as Occultism or Spiritual Philosophy. Remember my test: "DOES THIS MAKE ME STRONG?" Apply the touch-stone, and then govern yourself accordingly. This is a word to the Wise—heed it!

THE PROOF.

Concluding this part of the subject, I would say that if any of you are disposed to question the correctness of my above statement, then you have but to examine the types of "psychics" seen on all sides. Are they not all hyper-impressionable; excessively sensitive; neurotic; hysterical; passive; negative people? Do they not become as mere psychic harps, upon which the passing mental breezes play, producing weird sounds? Remember, now, I am speaking of genuine psychics, not the bogus psychics, who "are out for the money," and who are a shrewd, cunning lot, far from being impressionable, and in reality using their mesmeric power to impress and influence the credulous persons coming under their influence. I am not alluding to these people, but to the poor, frail-willed, negative sensitives, who are as impressionable as the photographer's "negative"—and to whom also the "development" means but the bringing out of impressions from outside. I pray you, be a HUMAN POSITIVE, not a HUMAN NEGATIVE!

CHAPTER XIII.

ORIENTAL FASCINATION.

At this point I wish to call your attention to a feature of the subject that has received but scant attention at the hands of Western writers. I allude to the wonderful manifestations of Mental Fascination displayed by some of the Magicians of the Orient, particularly of India and Persia. These feats are being performed today in those lands and are equal to any of the wonderful instances related of the ancient Persian or Egyptian Magicians.

MENTAL FASCINATION IN THE EAST.

Without going into an extended consideration of the subject in question I will mention a few of the recorded instances of Mental Fascination among the Oriental people, in order to give you an idea of the degree of power possible to an adept in the practice of Mental Influence. One writer describes an exhibition of this kind in India, witnessed by himself. The writer was a profound skeptic, who believed that it was all "hanky-panky" along the lines of sleight-of-hand or similar methods—that is, he so believed until he actually witnessed the demonstration. He goes on to relate that the Magician was a native Hindu, of dignified and imposing appearance, surrounded by a number of assistants of his own race.

THE SERPENT FEAT.

The Magician seated himself on the ground, with several jars, boxes, implements, and other paraphernalia before him. He opened the seance by the production of a number of tiny snakes, which he lifted from one of the boxes, and placed on the ground before him, in full sight of the audience, after allowing the latter to examine the serpents and thereby satisfy themselves regarding their reality. An English naturalist present identified the snakes as belonging to a well known native variety. The Magician then began a slow, mournful, droning, monotonous song, the predominant sound of which was "*um-m-m-m-m-m-m-m*," like the droning of a bumble bee or a distant saw mill. The snakes reared themselves up and moved their heads from side to side at the sound of the chant, the Magician touching them softly with his wand from time to time. To the eyes of the audience the snakes seemed to gradually grow from their original tiny proportions until finally they appeared as immense boa constrictors, which caused great alarm among the audience, both Englishmen and native. The Magician bade the audience remain quiet and assured them that there was no danger—then he reversed the process, and the snakes were seen to gradually decrease in size until they vanished from sight altogether.

THE VANISHING HINDU.

The next act was equally as wonderful. The Magician placed one of his assistants in the center of a circle described on the sand, and with appropriate gestures and ceremony went through some magical incantation. The boy was then seen to spin around, faster and faster, like a large top, and then began to gradually ascend in the air, still spinning around, until he vanished from sight. Then the Magician reversed the process and brought him down from the aerial heights, the boy appearing like a small speck at first, gradually growing larger as he neared the earth, until he stood before the audience, bowing and smiling.

THE MANGO FEAT.

The next act was the placing of some mango seeds in the sand, building a tiny hillock around them. The Magician then began his chant and waved his hands over the hillock. In a moment a tiny shoot was seen to appear, and then a little bush which gradually grew up until a mature mango tree was seen, bearing leaves. Then blossoms were seen, and the ripe fruit appeared, which was passed among the audience. Then, reversing the process, the tree disappeared gradually, and at the end the Magician dug up the original seeds and showed them to his audience. And, wonderful to relate, the fruit that had been distributed among the people also disappeared.

THE ROPE FEAT.

The concluding act was as startling as those preceding it. The Magician produced a coil of real rope, which was passed around for examination. Then he knotted one end of it and then tossed the knot into the air. The rope rapidly uncoiled itself, and the knot was seen away up in the air, and still ascending. When the rope was completely uncoiled, and the end left dangling on the ground as if supported by some hook holding the knotted end hundreds of feet up in the air, one of the assistants approached the rope and took hold of it. At a shout from the Magician he began climbing rapidly up the rope, and in a short time disappeared from view, after appearing as a tiny speck in the air. Then at another word from the Magician the rope itself flew up in the air and vanished from sight.

THE TEST AND EXPLANATION.

This concluded the performance. But here is a remarkable sequel. An Englishman present took a snapshot with a pocket camera, just as the boy began to climb the rope. *When the negative was developed there was no trace of rope, boy or anything else appertaining to the manifestation.* Even the Magician was absent from the center of the scene and was shown on the plate as sitting down on one side, with an amused smile on his face. This fact demonstrated that which similar tests have also proven; *i. e.*, that *the feats were not really performed at all* but were *simply illusions produced by impressions upon the minds of the audience.* In fact, they were examples of Mental Magic, along the phase of Mental Fascination, and arising from Concentrated Will, and Visualization of Mental Images, transmitted by Mentative Currents, and acting by Mentative Induction. I shall give you another proof of this in a moment or two, after I have related a few more instances of this wonderful manifestation of Mental Influence.

A WONDERFUL MAN.

Another writer, a correspondent of an American paper, relates that he was once on a steamer plying up one of the rivers in India, when, at a stopping place, there scrambled up the side as nimbly as a monkey a native Hindu, clad only in a loin cloth and having a tight-rolled red bundle fastened at the back of his neck to keep it safe from the water while swimming from shore. There was nothing about the man to distinguish him from the ordinary fakirs, but he soon showed his quality.

HIS STARTLING FEATS.

Passing along the deck he picked up a ball of thin rope which was lying there, and, unwinding an end, he knotted it and tossed the knot up in the air, where it ascended, rapidly unwinding the ball, until the whole of the rope disappeared in the air, just as in the instance previously related. Then passing a sailor who was holding in his hand a broken cocoanut shell containing the liquid or "water" of the nut, he lifted the shell from his hand and holding it high up over a ship's bucket standing nearby he emptied the liquid until it filled the bucket, and repeated the process upon another bucket, and so on until twelve buckets had been filled from the half-cocoanut shell. Then he picked up one of the buckets filled with the liquid and, holding it in his hand, he caused it to gradually shrink until it completely disappeared. Then a moment later he exhibited a tiny speck in his hand, which gradually grew until it was again the bucket of water filled to the brim with the liquid, which he then poured out on the deck.

A STRANGE OCCURRENCE.

Witnessing the strange performance was a young mother with her babe beside her and a young nurse girl several feet away. To her horror the mother then beheld the nurse girl rising a few feet in the air and moving rapidly toward the babe, reaching down for the infant as she glided over it, and then rising high into the air with the child clasped in her arms, until both were lost in the clouds. The mother burst into frantic cries and shrieks and gazed upward; and as she gazed she saw a fleecy cloud appear, which gradually took the shape of the nurse girl, who grew larger and larger as she descended, until she finally reached the deck again and handed the babe to the rejoiced mother. The mother, after clasping her babe close to her bosom, cried out, "How dare you take my child away?" when to her surprise the girl answered, "Why, ma'am, the baby has been asleep all the time and I have not touched him." And then the fakir smiled and said, "Mem Sahib has only been dreaming strange things." It was merely an instance of Mental Impression of a remarkable degree of power produced by the Will and Mental Imagery of the fakir; and his previous feats were also so performed.

WONDERS UPON WONDERS.

But this was only the beginning. The fakir then untied his red bundle, and, extracting therefrom a cocoanut, he exhibited it to the passengers, passing it around for inspection. Then, placing the nut on the end of a bamboo stick, and, balancing it there, he commanded it in *Hindi* to spout as a fountain, and immediately a great jet of water sprang from it, falling over the deck in great showers. He then caused it to stop flowing, and it obeyed; then he restarted it. This he repeated several times. Then he materialized a cobra from the air and caused it to disappear at his command, after he had terrified the passengers with it. Then he materialized several human forms in broad sunlight in full view of the passengers, and afterwards caused them to melt away gradually until they disappeared like a cloud of steam. Then taking up a collection, which was quite liberal, he jumped over the side and swam rapidly to shore.

THE REAL SECRET.

The natives among the ship's passengers smiled at the wonder of the Europeans present and laughed at the latter's talk of jugglery or magic power, informing them that it was merely an instance of Hindu Mesmerism, or Mental Influence, and that those among them who resisted the spell saw nothing of the phenomena, except the fakir with glistening eyes, and every evidence of a powerful and concentrated exercise of his Will. These feats are quite common in some parts of India, but they are known to be but mental illusions, for all attempts to catch the exhibition on photographic plates have failed, the plate showing nothing but the magician in a state of mental concentration. These magicians have developed the power of causing many persons, at the same time, to have the illusion of seeing, hearing, tasting and smelling things that have no material existence. It is Induced Mental Imagery in a developed degree, but differs only in degree from the phenomena more familiar to the Western World.

TESTIMONY OF A HINDU SAGE.

In this connection I would like to add the testimony and explanation given to me personally by a greatly esteemed friend of mine—a Hindu sage—traveling in this country, who in addition to his Oriental learning has received the highest English education and who is "a highly educated man" in both the Eastern and Western meanings of the terms. This gentleman told me that when a youth he had witnessed exhibitions of the kind just related in his native land. At first he was puzzled and mystified by them, but his naturally scientific turn of mind caused him to seek for the solution. He began experimenting, and soon at least was able to classify the phenomena as pure Mental Illusion. He found that the crowd would gather close around the Magician in order to see what was going on, although all were required to keep a certain number of yards away from the wonder-worker by the latter's instructions and requirements. My friend found that if he retreated a few yards beyond the outer edge of the crowd *he could see nothing but the magician,* all the "magical doings" disappearing. When he would join the crowd the mystic appearances were again plainly seen. He tried the experiment in several ways, with the same result. Then he tried a riskier one and pushed nearer to the magician than was allowable—and with the same result. In short, the influence was confined to a certain area and the mental influence was doubtless increased by the "contagion" of the different minds in the crowd. My friend tested the well-known "Mango feat" and the "Rope-disappearing feat" (as related in these pages) in this way and determined that they came well under the rule of "Mental Illusion," instead of being an occurrence defying the established laws of Nature. The testimony of this gentleman corroborated the opinion that I had already formed to that effect, which opinion agrees with that of the best authorities.

AN ERRONEOUS WESTERN IDEA.

In closing this chapter I wish to point out to the students of the work an erroneous idea that has crept into some of the Western works along the lines of hypnotism, etc., and which I shall now mention and explain. The Hindu magicians, or mesmerists, frequently sit in a squatting position during their "enchantments," droning a monotonous, soothing chant, as has been described, and at the same time moving the body from the waist upward, in a circling, twisting motion, from the hips, at the same time fixing their gaze firmly upon their audience. This motion and twisting is merely an accompaniment to the droning chant akin to the motions of the Oriental dancers who twist their bodies in a similar manner in rhythm to the music. The motion is merely a custom among these people and has nothing to do with the production of the phenomena, as all Hindu Occultists know and will tell you. In fact, the higher magicians among the Hindus do nothing of the sort, but maintain a dignified, calm, standing position, or the firm "Yogi seat," in which the body is evenly and firmly poised in a position of dignified rest, the hands resting on the lap, the back of one hand in the palm of the other.

A FOOLISH IDEA.

All native Hindus understand the above matter, but Western visitors jump at the conclusion that this gyrating circling of the body from the hips has something to do with the "power" manifested. And, as I have said, some of the Western works on the subject have gone into considerable detail regarding this wonderful "Oriental Hypnotism," which they assert is accomplished because of this twisting of the body. They might just as well point out some physical trick of motion of each leading Western hypnotist and assert that the motion was the "secret of his power." I do not think that further comment is necessary in this case. The motions and attitudes, etc., are merely part of the setting of the piece, or possibly bits of "stage business," designed to heighten the impression of mystery. That's all.

ORIENTAL METHODS OF DEVELOPING POWER.

I have been informed by an authority whose word is entitled to the greatest respect, and who has spent many years in India and other Oriental countries, that the following method is used by these Oriental Magicians in developing within themselves the power to create these strong Mental Images in the minds of those witnessing their performances: The Magician starts when a youth and practices Mental Imagery in his own mind. This process is akin to Visualization, as mentioned by me in my work on Mental Magic. The Magician at first uses his Will in an endeavor to form a clear and distinct mental image of some familiar object, a rose, for instance. He practices until he is able to actually *see the thing before him "in his mind's eye,"* just as certain eminent painters have acquired the faculty of "visualizing" the faces of persons they meet, so that they can reproduce them on canvas without further sittings.

SUPERLATIVE SENSE-INDUCTION ATTAINED.

Then the Magician experiments upon larger objects, and then upon groups of objects, and so on to more complex pictures.

After years of constant experimentation and practice a few of those undertaking the work find themselves able to picture any of the scenes described in this chapter as "feats"—that is, they are able to clearly picture them in their own minds. And this being accomplished, the Magician is able by his highly-developed Concentrated Will to project the Mental Image into the mind of those around him. It is the Sense Induction, described by me in this work, only raised to a much higher degree of manifestation.

ORIENTAL VS. OCCIDENTAL.

The people of the West will not devote the time and attention to the cultivation of such faculties, while the Oriental will willingly give up half of his life for the attainment. But, on the other hand, the Western man will devote his time to the acquirement of Will Power and Concentration in the direction of becoming a Ruler of Men and a General of Finance. Each to his taste and temperament—and neither would "trade" places or power with the other. They are both dealing with the same Force, however, as little as they realize it.

CHAPTER XIV.

FUTURE-IMPRESSION.

I now wish to call your attention to what may be called "Future-Impression," or, as the hypnotists call it; "post-hypnotism," etc. Future-Impressions are like seeds planted in the mind, which grow, blossom and bear fruit at some future time. The hypnotists produce this phenomena by giving the subject while in the hypnotic sleep (?) the suggestion that at a certain time, either in a few minutes, or hours, or days, he will *do* certain things, or *feel* certain things. But the newer school of psychologists have discovered that these Future-Impressions may be made in the ordinary receptive state, just as is the case with any of the other forms of Mental Impressions, and the result will be the same as that obtained by the hypnotists, in spite of their theories and methods.

THE GENERAL PRINCIPLES.

I do not purpose going into detail regarding this class of phenomena, because all that is necessary to be said can be comprised in the following two statements:

(1) *That, generally speaking, all the phenomena of the ordinary immediate Mental Impression may be produced as Future-Impression;* and (2) *that all the phenomena of Future-Impression, produced by the operator on the subject, may be likewise produced by auto-impression of the subject (that is, by the subject inducing impressions in himself).*

HOW FUTURE-IMPRESSIONS ARE GIVEN.

In the first of the above stated principles the subject is merely told that, "You will do so and so, at such and such a time," instead of "Do so and so now." For instance, instead of telling the "*impressionable*" that the chair is burning him now, you may tell him that in two minutes he will feel the chair burning him—the result will be similar in both cases. Apply the same principle to any of the mesmeric phenomena mentioned in previous chapters and the result will be similar. The force of the impression, the degree of impressionability, etc., will play the same part in both Immediate Impression and Future Impression. This principle is called into operation by Suggestionists in treating for "habits," the suggestions being given along the lines of "Every time you pick up a cigar you will feel nauseated and will think of a disgusting bar-room spittoon," etc., etc. It is always a case of "you *will*" in Future Impression.

INSTANCES FROM EVERYDAY LIFE.

Many foolish suggestions are given in everyday life along the lines of Future Impression, and alas! many of them are accepted carelessly, owing to a lack of knowledge of the principle. How many times has it been said to an impressionable young bride, "Never mind, you'll grow tired of him after a while," etc. Or to a man, "Wait until the novelty wears off and you'll see how sick of the job you'll get." Or, "You'll lose your interest and enthusiasm, bye-and-bye." Or, "You'll find him out after a while and will see that he's not what he seems." And so on—you may add to these instances from your own experience. And too often these suggestions are recalled and have a tendency to cause the person to "make them come true." Many fortune-tellers' prophecies have been made come true in this way by impressionable and ignorant people. I have given you a key to this principle now—heed the lesson! If you feel that an attempt at Future Impression is being made on you head it off with a mental "*No, I Wont!*" That is the Antidote for the Bane. Remember this—it may save you trouble some day!

THE SECRET OF FUTURE AUTO-IMPRESSIONS.

The second principle in the statement made several paragraphs further back—*i. e.*, that all the phenomena of Future Impression may be duplicated by Auto-Impression, or Impressions made by one's self—is true and worthy of consideration. You make up your mind that you must awaken to catch a train at four tomorrow morning—and you awaken in time. You have set your mental alarm clock. If you have an engagement at three this afternoon you may set your alarm as follows (talking to yourself, of course): Now, see here! Remember that you must see Smith at three this afternoon—three, *three,* I say! Remember now, THREE, I say!" And if you impress it sufficiently strong upon your mind, a little before three you will begin to feel uneasy, and then suddenly your Smith engagement will "pop" into your mind from your subconscious region, and you will reach out for your hat and overcoat. Mental Alarm-clock, remember! That tells the whole tale.

THE MENTAL ALARM CLOCK.

You see, the experimenter giving Future Impressions simply sets the Mental Alarm-clock going along "impressionable" lines. He makes the Mental Impression and attaches it to the Mental Alarm Clock—when the Alarm goes off the Impression emerges into the field of consciousness and acts just as if it had been freshly made. That's the whole story in plain homely terms.

SELF-PROTECTION.

But don't be frightened, you timid people. Remember this, that you will not accept a Future Impression unless you would also accept a Present Impression—the degree of "impressionability" is the same in both cases. The only reason a Future Impression has the advantage over a present one is that it is more subtle, and people are not as much on guard about future things as they are about things to be "done right now." You will resent an impression that you "Do this thing right Now," while you pay but little attention to the earnest impression that "in a year from now you will feel so-and-so about this matter," and dismiss the subject with a shrug of the shoulders, instead of saying, at least mentally, *"No, I Wont!"* The present impression is apt to attract your attention the more forcibly, because it is more apparent—while the Future Impression is more "insinuating." But now that you know the facts of the matter you may laugh at them both, and *take the sting out of them* by your little *"No, I Wont"!*

HOW TO KILL OUT OLD ADVERSE IMPRESSIONS.

And, just one word more. If you feel that you are harboring any Future Impressions made on you in the past, but upon which the Alarm has not yet gone off, you may kill them by direct Self-Impression, or Auto-Suggestions to the contrary. That is, you may say "I WILL NOT act upon any adverse Impressions that may have been made to me—I WILL them out of my mind—I KILL THEM this moment by the power of my WILL." And at the same time make a Mental Picture of the Impression being obliterated by the action of your Will, just as the chalk mark is erased from the blackboard by the passing over it of the eraser. Try this plan and be Free! Some of you will thank me for this, mark my words.

CHAPTER XV.

ESTABLISHING A MENTATIVE CENTRE.

We now approach that part of this work in which each individual student is called upon to decide for himself whether or not he wishes to take his place in the world as a Live, Active Centre of Mentative Energy, or whether he wishes to remain a Negative, Passive, Half-Alive Centre. No matter which plan you may choose, you cannot avoid being a Centre of some kind—the question for you to decide is, "What kind of a Centre do I wish to become?"

EACH INDIVIDUAL A CENTRE.

I have explained in my work on "Mental Magic," and again in the first chapter of the present work, that each individual is a Centre of Life, Energy and Force in the Great Ocean of Universal Mentative Energy. Each Individual is a Centre around which revolves his own world, be that world great or small. The principle is the same in all cases. And each man's world is largely what he makes it—what he attracts to himself. From the time that the child begins to assert the "I" in him he begins to create for himself his world. He draws this person and thing, and repels that person or thing, in accordance with his mental nature. And he is constantly changing his little world according to the growth of his nature.

MENTAL WORLD-BUILDING.

In view of this law of life, does it not become of importance to us to begin to build our mental world with care, and with the best possible material? Should we not begin to make ourselves active Centres of Energy, that we may have the necessary Power to build strongly and well? Should we not develop within us our Powers of Attraction, that we may draw to us the things, persons and circumstances that are conducive to our well-being and content? Should we not develop the Will-Power within us, in order to exert that Force which is necessary to push our way through the tangled underbrush of Life and make a wide path for ourselves? Answer these questions as you will. I have answered them for myself, and you must do the same for yourselves.

THE IMPORTANT DECISION.

And so I shall proceed with this work with the understanding that you have answered my questions in the affirmative and have decided to Create an Active Mentative Centre for Yourself. If you have decided in the negative you might as well close this book, for from now on the instruction will be along the lines above indicated.

THE DUAL FORCE.

Let us pause for a moment and see what Forces are combined in this Active Mentative Centre. In the first place we see that the dual aspect of the Mental Energy manifests itself always. That which we have called the Desire-Force, and that which we have called the Will-Power, appear as the Two Mentative Poles. You know this well, for you have studied my main work on "Mental Magic," wherein this point is brought out and illustrated. But here is an aspect of the matter that I did not take the time to bring out at great length in the said book. I allude to the resemblance of the two phases of Mentative Energy, *i. e.*, Desire-Force and Will-Power, to the physical phenomena of Magnetism and Electricity respectively.

PHYSICAL LAWS IN THE MENTAL WORLD.

Desire-Force, like Magnetism, manifests in a drawing, pulling, attracting power; while Will-Power, like Electricity, manifests in a pushing, compelling, driving power. Desire-Force, like Magnetism, tends to draw things inward and to itself; while Will-Power, like Electricity, tends to drive things outward and away from itself. This dual manifestation of Energy is seen all through Nature in all of its manifold forms and conditions. There is ever the drawing in to a centre—and there is ever the pushing outward from the centre. And this Law manifests upon the Mental Plane as well as upon the Physical Plane.

MENTAL ELECTRO-MAGNETISM.

We have heard much of people being "Magnetic," that is, having the power to attract persons to them—but that is merely one phase of the operation of Mentative Energy. We do not hear so much about people being "Electric," and yet the term is just as proper and applicable as the term "Magnetic." "Electric" people are the people in whom Will-Power is strongly developed and manifest. These people "get after" others and make them do things. They are the active, energetic, forceful men and women who "get behind things" and push them along. All great leaders possess this phase of Energy to a marked degree. The mere mention of the matter to you will cause you to think of instances of people who possess Mentative "Electricity." There are men who are able to make the crowd around them do their bidding—they are able to work their Will upon the mass of people. These men are seen to possess a strange power, but very few understand it. It is entirely different from the fascinating, alluring, charming, attractive personality of the "Magnetic" man, for it forces, and compels by sheer force of character and Will, instead of drawing and attracting. You will see why I have spoken of these two phases as Masculine and Feminine respectively when you consider their different manner of manifestation.

THE ELECTRO-MAGNETIC INDIVIDUAL.

But, while both of these forms of Power, the "Magnetic" and the "Electric," have their strong points and advantages, I hold that the highly developed Individual must have both of these phases developed highly. In short, instead of being merely a very "Magnetic" individual, on the one hand, or a very "Electric" individual, on the other hand, the ideal man must be an ELECTRO-MAGNETIC INDIVIDUAL. In other words, he must have both sides of his Mentative Energy highly developed and in full operation. In this way he is able to manifest a combined influence which will make him a very giant of Mentative Energy.

FROM THEORY TO PRACTICE.

Now I have said enough about the theory of the thing. I shall ask you to read over what I have said above several times—in fact re-read it until you thoroughly understand it. And then I shall take you on to the practical work and exercises calculated to develop in you the qualities mentioned. Taking it for granted that you have carefully considered what I have just said, I shall ask you to perform the following exercises, etc.:

FIRST EXERCISE FOR REALIZING THE CENTRE.

EXERCISE I. In order to realize the reality of the statement that you are a Centre of Mentative Power you must first enter into a realization of the existence of a Great Ocean of Mentative Energy itself. Do not pass over this lightly, for it is most important. You must begin to create a Mental Picture of the Universe as a Great Ocean of Living Energy, vibrating with Life and Force and Power. Endeavor to make this Mental Picture so clear that you can "see it with your mind's eye," and until it becomes a reality to you. Picture yourself *as alone in the Universe* and surrounded on all sides with a vibrating, pulsating sea of Energy, or Power. See that ALL POWER is locked up in that ocean, and that the ocean exists EVERYWHERE. Cut out from your Mental Field all other persons, things or conditions. *Imagine yourself as alone in the great Ocean of Power.* You must practice frequently upon this Mental Picture until you are able to visualize it distinctly. This does not mean that you have to actually *see* it, just as you do this printed page; but that you should be able to actually *feel* it. You will begin to understand just what I mean after you have practiced this a little. This Great Ocean of Universal Power must become REAL to you—and you must practice until it does so become.

THE IMPORTANCE OF THE EXERCISE.

The importance of the above exercise may be understood when I tell you that it will be impossible for you to manifest more than a moderate degree of Power until you are able to realize yourself as a real Centre. And it will be impossible for you to realize yourself as such a Centre until you realize the existence of the Ocean of Power itself. For how can you think of yourself as a Centre of Power, in an Ocean of Power, until you realize the existence of the Ocean itself? The Universal Ocean of Mentative Energy contains within itself *all* the Power, Force and Energy that there is. It is the source from which all forms of Energy arise. It is filled with an infinite number of tiny Centres of Energy, of which YOU are one. And in the degree that you draw upon it for Strength, so will you receive Strength. By all means endeavor to clearly visualize this Great Mentative Ocean, for it is the source of all the Force with which you are filled and which you hope to acquire. Enter into this Great Realization, friends, for it is *The First Step to Power.*

SECOND EXERCISE FOR REALIZING THE CENTRE.

EXERCISE II. The second exercise, which will tend to increase your vibration as a Centre of Force, is as follows: Picture yourself clearly as a CENTRE OF FORCE in the Mentative Ocean. While seeing the Ocean on all sides of you, you must see yourself as *the Centre of it.* Do not be frightened at this idea, for it is based on the Truth. The highest Occult Teaching informs us that the Great Mentative Ocean *has its centre Everywhere and its circumference Nowhere.* That is, that being Infinite in Space, there is no finite spot that is *really* its Centre, and yet, on the other hand, every Point of Activity may be called its Centre. Being extended in every direction infinitely, its circumference is nonexistent. Therefore you are entitled and justified in considering yourself as a Centre of the Ocean of Power. Each Individual is such a Centre, and each has his world circling and revolving around him. Some have a small world, and some have mighty ones. There are Centres so mighty and exalted that the human mind cannot grasp their importance. But even the tiniest Point of Activity is a Centre in Itself. So hesitate not, but begin to form a Mental Picture of yourself as a CENTRE OF POWER.

A FOCAL POINT OF FORCE.

Practice this exercise until you can clearly *feel*

yourself as a Centre of Power. You must learn to think of yourself as a Focal Point of Force in the Great Mentative Ocean. Just as the great body of Electricity manifests itself in tiny points of activity, so does the Mentative Energy so express itself in YOU who are a Point of Activity within Itself. In urging you to perfect yourself in this realization I would impress upon you the fact, known to all advanced Occultists, that in the measure of your realization of this Real Nature of the Ego will be the measure of the Power possessed by You. All of the Strong Men of our times, and of all ages, had this realization, intuitively or instinctively; that is, although they did not know the philosophy or science of the matter, they still *felt,* and *feel,* this sense of the Power of the Ego in themselves, which gives them the confidence to do things and the Will-Power and Desire-Force to carry out their undertakings. It is this feeling of Inherent Strength that makes men Strong and Successful and Positive. And this feeling and realization may be developed and unfolded within any one, providing he *wants it "sufficiently hard."* By the exercise of your Desire and Will you may build up this realization of Power, and in the building up there will come to you a constantly increasing stream of Desire and Will. In the measure of your Expression will be the measure of your Impression from the Source of All Positive Impression.

THIRD EXERCISE FOR REALIZING THE CENTRE.

EXERCISE III. The third exercise consists in the realization of the Nature of the Force. This Force, Energy or Power with which you are being filled, and which you are now attracting toward your Centre, consists of the Electrical Manifestation of Will-Power and the Magnetic Manifestation of Desire-Force. These two constitute the Dual Phases of the One Force. And, therefore, you must begin to realize that these qualities are within you in order that you may be able to express the same and thus gain the addition and increased Force that comes to those who Express the same. You must begin to realize that you have a WILL which is capable of impressing itself on the things, persons and circumstances of your world—and you must begin to realize that you have a DESIRE which attracts to you the things, people and circumstances of your world, and which, in fact, draws to you the very material from which your world is made. When you realize this dual force within you, it will begin to express itself automatically. The act of realization causes the mental machinery to begin to work smoothly and effectively. Therefore picture to yourself this Dual Force within you. See yourself as influencing, and acting upon the world around you. See yourself as a Power in the land. And also see yourself as an Attracting Force, drawing to you that which you need and want and require, consciously and unconsciously. Picture yourself as *an Electro-Magnetic Individual.* You are an Individual because you are a Centre of Power. You are Electro-Magnetic because you possess the Electric Will and the Magnetic Desire.

A STRONG STATEMENT.

Carry with you this thought constantly and repeat it often to yourself and you will find it a source of Strength—you will find the Strength pouring into you when you say or think it. When you feel weak, or when you feel the need of additional Strength, use this Statement of Strength:

"I AM A LIVING ELECTRO-MAGNET."

And when you say it, or think it, you must picture to yourself just what you mean by the statement, hence the importance of knowing *just what is meant.* Do not pass over this Statement of Strength as unimportant, but try it in actual practice and you will soon see what a Battery of Strength it will be for you. And those around you will soon become aware of a new sense of Power Within you.

DON'T LEAN ON OTHERS—DON'T LET OTHERS LEAN ON YOU.

Keep this Statement to yourself. Do not invite the

ridicule of those around you by telling them the Source of your Strength. Do not bother about them—if they are Individuals themselves they will understand without being told; and if they are not, why, all the telling in the world would not make it clear to them. Hoe your own row and mind your own business—and let them do the same. No one can build up his Individuality except from Within. And each must work out his own salvation and climb the Ladder of Attainment for himself. And the sooner that people learn this the better will it be for all. Don't be a Leaner, or a Leaning-post. Don't lean on anyone else—and don't let anyone lean on you.

LIVE YOUR OWN LIFE AND LET OTHERS LIVE THEIRS.

There has been too much of this fool business about living other people's lives for them, or letting other people live your life for you. Each man or woman must grow into an Individual by his or her own work and life. There is no such thing as vicarious Individuality. Don't be afraid to "assert the I"—to claim your rightful heritage and birthright to be an Individual, and not a Parasite. And don't be afraid to shake off and trim off the parasitic persons that have encumbered your own unfoldment toward Individuality. Let the Parasites take root in the earth, just as you have done; let them fasten their roots in the great body of Strength and Power instead of in the mental body of someone else; let them stop their second-hand nourishment and learn to draw from the First Source. This is the only way, and the lack of the knowledge of it is filling the world with weaklings instead of with Individuals.

Therefore think of these things; hold them well in mind when you make your Statement of Strength:

"I AM A LIVING ELECTRO-MAGNET."

CHAPTER XVI.

PERSONAL ATMOSPHERE.

The Mentative Force emanating from each individual creates a Mental Atmosphere around him which often extends a considerable distance from his body, especially in the case of strong individuals, whose Mental Atmosphere is felt when they enter a room or public place. Persons whose personality is weaker have a Mental Atmosphere extending only a few inches from their bodies, and which is scarcely perceptible to those coming in contact with them.

THE POSITIVE AURA.

The man of Positive Individuality—our man who feels himself to be a "Living Electro-Magnet"—carries with him an aura of Mental Atmosphere of Positive Strength, which is plainly felt by those coming in contact with him. People say about such a man that he "has something about him" which impresses them, but which they fail to understand. It will be worth your while to study this Mental Atmosphere of some strong man with whom you come in contact, for now that you have the secret of the matter you may take some valuable lessons from him.

THE "AIR ABOUT" STRONG INDIVIDUALS.

As I have said in my "Mental Magic:" "I cannot very well describe this 'air' to you, for unless you have met a man of this kind you will not understand it. But it is a very different thing from the pompous, self-sufficient, self-important, fussy air and demeanor manifested by the cheap imitators of these great men. The Magnetic Man does not tell you how great, or smart, or important he is—he leaves that for his cheap imitators; he makes you feel his strength by his very manner and atmosphere, without saying a word. He has that 'something about him' that people notice and wonder at. And that 'something' comes from his conscious or unconscious relation to the Universal Will."

INDIVIDUALITY NOT PERSONALITY.

In the above paragraph I have pointed out to the student the kernel of the matter. The "little fellow" who thinks he is one of the "big ones" believes that his strength comes from his Personality, and sooner or later he trips himself up because of this error. But the real "big ones" of life know better; they may not understand it all, but some way they feel that there is a "Something" back of them from which they are able to draw Strength and Power, and believing this, they are filled with Courage and Daring and radiate their Strength on all sides. They may talk of their "lucky star" or "special providence," or else believe themselves to be "specially favored of God" (as is the case with at least one of the "big men" of modern finance), but no matter what may be their special interpretations of this "Something," they all recognize its existence and trust to it. And this conviction and realization gives to the strong individuals that air of calm, positive Power and Self-Confidence that impresses those with whom they come in contact and which forms their Mental Atmosphere.

BACK TO FIRST PRINCIPLES.

And in giving you instructions in the art of building for yourselves a positive Mental Atmosphere I can do no better than to refer you back to first principles and again bid you to realize that you are a Dynamic Focus—a Centre of Force—in the great Universal Will, having the dual attribute of Will-Power and Desire-Force. In short, that you are A LIVING ELECTRO-MAGNET.

REALIZATION BRINGS POWER.

If you will but get this realization firmly fixed in your mind you will automatically create for yourself a most positive Mental Atmosphere that will be felt by all with whom you come in contact. So first, last and all the time build up this Realization. Say to yourself, "I am a Living Electro-Magnet;" think it out; dream it out; act it out. And, of course, always realize what all this means. You are the Electro-Magnet through which is pouring the Universal Will-Power, and in the degree that you *allow the current to so flow through you,* so will be the Power you are able to manifest.

HOW TO USE THE REALIZATION.

When you wish to manifest a special degree of Power just let this Statement flame out in vivid letters in your mind. When you feel that you are being approached by some other person of strong will, whom you do not wish to influence you, just bring this Statement into effect, and you will actually see the effect of it upon the other person. He will feel your strong Mental Atmosphere and will cease to try to affect you. And even when there is no special need for making the Statement of Power it will be well for you to keep it burning bright within you, for by so doing you strengthen your realization, and your Mental Atmosphere reflects the inner mental state.

SPECIAL MENTAL ATMOSPHERES.

So much for the General Mental Atmosphere. As we proceed we shall see that the Electro-Magnetic Individual creates special Mental Atmospheres around him by his Mental States, depending upon his Will or Desire at the time. Not only does his Will and Desire affect other persons directly by means of Mental Currents, but Mentative Induction is also set up by the Mental Atmosphere, without any special effort on his part.

MAINTAIN YOUR POSITIVITY.

In this place I wish to call your attention to the importance of always maintaining your Positivity as a means of Mental Training. Do not allow yourself to become negative to others, even where there is nothing lost by so doing, for by this neglect you create a negative habit which will cause you trouble to overcome later. If a person comes into your presence whose personality seems likely to dominate or overpower yours, by all means interpose a mental resistance right then and there. It is not necessary for you to manifest the same in words, for that would make you ridiculous in many cases; nor is it necessary for you to give any special physical expression to your mental state. Simply look the person in the eye, carelessly and without any special effort, at the same time making the mental statement, "I Am A Living Electro-Magnet," and you will find that your Positivity will rise until it is equal with his, and your feeling of negativity will disappear. In exceptional cases you may add mentally, "I am as Positive as You."

HOW TO CREATE POSITIVE AURAS.

It will be well for you to practice the creation of special mental Atmospheres in order to establish the habit and thus render it easier to avail yourself of the same on special occasions. Opportunities of all kinds will present themselves to you in everyday life. The gist of the matter is to surround yourself with a Mental Aura of such a nature that people will act toward you as you wish them to do. A few examples may help you to get a clearer idea of what I mean, so I herewith give you the same.

AN INTERESTING EXAMPLE.

I know a lady, living in Chicago, who was constantly complaining that people were "always running over her" on State Street (the crowded retail street of the great Western metropolis). She said that they were always crowding her off the sidewalk and pushing, bumping and jostling her in a most annoying manner. She asked me for instructions as to what thought she should use to prevent individuals from so acting. I answered that I did not think it was necessary to consider the separate individuals in the case, but that she should "treat" *the crowd as a whole*, by means of a protective Mental Atmosphere. I then advised her to build up a Mental Atmosphere around this Statement: "People respect my rights; they will not unduly impose on me in the street; I deny the Power of the Crowd to impose on me." And she followed this advice, and in a short time had built up a Protective Mental Atmosphere which acted almost magically upon the crowd, who stepped aside and gave her a full right-of-way on the pavement. She would simply go on her way calmly, serenely and undisturbed, and *the crowd let her alone.* I must add that I think that the original trouble arose from a subconscious dislike to the crowds and an extreme shrinking from people, the result being that this dislike acted almost as does Fear, and really attracted to her the interference of people. The new Mental Atmosphere dispelled the old one and gave her an additional Positivity besides.

FEAR AS AN ATTRACTING FORCE.

In this connection I would call your attention to that remarkable psychological fact that *Fear acts as an attracting force*, in a negative way. If you *want* a thing very much you attract it to you—and if you *fear* it very much you do likewise. This apparent contradiction has bothered many students of the subject, but it seems very plain to me. I think the explanation is that in both cases a vivid Mental Picture is held, and the attraction results along the line of

Visualization, which always tends to Materialize the Mental Image. Do you see what I mean? Think over it a bit and you will see it plainly.

THE TRANSFORMATION OF A "HUMAN DOOR-MAT."

Another case, from actual experience. Another lady, also a resident of Chicago, complained that the clerks in the great department stores would not treat her courteously, but would keep her waiting without paying her any attention, and in other ways would treat her like a "human door-mat." She said she would not have minded this so much if other women were treated likewise, but that while she was ignored others would receive the greatest attention, the clerks "falling over themselves" to wait upon them. I told her that she had gradually built up around her a Mental Atmosphere of Expectancy—that she had fallen into the habit of *expecting such treatment,* and consequently she got what she expected. I think that in the beginning she had manifested a timid, "humble," meek, "worm-of-the-dust" state of mind when she entered the big stores, which somewhat overawed her. And then, after this drew upon her the neglect of the clerks, who seem very ready to wipe their feet on human door-mats, she grew to regularly expect the shabby treatment. It was not a matter of dress, or anything of that kind, for she dressed well —and, for that matter, I know women who dress poorly who never get any such treatment, for they understand the underlying mental laws too well for that. It was simply a matter of a Negative Mental Atmosphere, as many of you will clearly see.

HOW THE CHANGE OCCURRED.

Well, I told her to "brace up" and create a new Mental Atmosphere, around this general Statement: "The clerks like me; they like to wait on me; they give me every attention; they do this *because they LIKE me,* and also because I INSIST UPON IT as my Right!" The charm worked in a short time, and now the good lady reports that the clerks not only treat her well but even take the trouble to call her attention to desirable selections, special bargains, and all the rest of it. The cure was perfect.

AN ANALYSIS.

I call your attention to the above Statement—please note that the first part of it operated along the lines of Desire-Force, and the latter part along the lines of Will-Power. The Statement of the first-mentioned lady (the one who objected to street-crowding) was altogether along the lines of Will-Power. I ask the students to study and dissect each of these cases, because by so doing they will be able to apply the principles in cases coming under their own observation, and also in their own cases.

THE LADY WHOM "NOBODY LOVED."

I once directed a lady who complained that she was unpopular, and that "nobody loved her," etc., etc., to apply a similar method. She created a new Mental Atmosphere around her along the lines of the general Statement: "People *like me;* they find me *attractive;* they *love me,* and *like to be in my company.*" After a time she reported that from a state of "wall-flowerdom" she had become quite a favorite, and in fact was at a loss to adjust herself to the changed conditions, finding somewhat of an embarrassment of "likings" and "lovings." This was a case of Desire-Force pure and simple.

MORE THAN WORDS NEEDED.

Now do not imagine for a moment that in the above cases, and hundreds of others known to me personally, the desired result was obtained merely from repeating, parrot-like, or like a phonograph, the words of the Statement. This talk of the Power of Mere Words, and all the rest of such talk, has made me very "tired" indeed. I have seen and heard so much of this nonsense since I have become acquainted with certain people who consider themselves "in the New Thought" that I dislike to use the words "Statement" or "Affirmation." These people have imagined that by the mere repetition of *words* they could work miracles. Pshaw! What nonsense! They remind me of the Chinese, and certain other people who write long prayers on slips of paper and allow them to flutter in the breeze, hoping that the gods will accept their prayers at face value while the prayer-makers are amusing themselves elsewhere. Sometimes they attach little bells to the prayers in order to attract the attention of the gods. Others paste the prayers on water-wheels, turned by the streams, thereby claiming credit for a prayer at each turn of the wheel. Cheap praying that! Oh, don't laugh—some of you are just as foolish. You have been making your Statements and Affirmations in the same spirit, and now feel disappointed because "nothing happened." Of course nothing happened; how could it be otherwise?

THE FEELING BEHIND THE WORDS.

I have said over and over again—and now say it over again another time—that the words of themselves are nothing; the real virtue lies in the feeling behind the words. If there is no feeling there is no result. In order to get the results you must erect the framework of words, and then build around it the structure of feeling, and expectation, and visualization. That's the way to do it. The words are merely the skeleton—the flesh and blood are the feelings and materialized visualizations.

GO AND DO LIKEWISE.

The ladies mentioned above, whom I have used as "typical cases" to illustrate the principle—they did not rest content with words, *for I wouldn't let them.* I kept after them, insisting upon their using the proper mental exercises and methods—that's what did the work. And now I shall give you the same instruction and directions that I gave them—adapt them to your own cases and you will be likewise successful.

THE KERNEL OF THE MATTER.

The kernel of the process of creating the Mental Atmosphere lies in what I have called "Visualization," and which I have described at length in my work on "Mental Magic." This Visualization is simply the creation of a strong Mental Image of the thing desired, and perfecting it each day until it becomes almost as clear as an existing material thing. Then the Visualization tends to Materialize itself—that is, it begins to build around itself actual material conditions corresponding with the mental framework. The Statement of words is the pattern around which the Visualized Mental Image forms itself. And the Mental Image is the framework around which the actual material conditions form themselves. Do you remember the instance of the Hindu Magician mentioned in a previous chapter? Well, that will give you the idea. The lady made her Mental Image of the street-conduct of the crowd—and the crowd unconsciously felt it and built themselves around it. So in the case of the lady in the department store, and the others mentioned. The Mental Image manifested itself as a Mental Atmosphere, and gradually materialized.

HOW TO VISUALIZE.

The thing to do in Visualizing is to bring the Positive Imagination to see and feel the thing as actually existent. Then by constant practice and meditation the Mental Atmosphere becomes formed, and the rest is all a matter of time. *See yourself as you wish to be. See others as you wish them to be. See conditions as you wish them to be.* Think them out—dream them out—act them out. And Materialization will follow upon Visualization, even as Visualization followed upon the Statement.

DEGREES OF RECEPTIVITY.

In this connection, however, I must call your attention to the fact that the degrees of receptivity of other people to your Mental Atmospheres and Mental Pictures depend entirely upon their degree of Positivity. They respond only in the degree that they respond to other mentative influences. The Strong avoid influences to which the Weak yield, in this as in every other phase of the phenomena. But do not let that cause fear on your part. You may make yourself Positive—you have had the instructions given you, and it is now "up to you" to do the rest.

READ BETWEEN THE LINES.

I might write a whole book on this subject of Visualization in the phase of forming Mental Atmospheres—but what would be the use? I have herein given you the underlying principles, and have also given you a few illustrative examples—you must do the rest yourselves. If you have carefully read this book, and have studied *between the lines* as well as the lines themselves, you will have grasped the little details of the matter which will not be apparent to those who have not done so. Each will find in this book that for which he or she is ready—and not a bit more. I think the careful students among you will readily understand just what I mean by this. If you do not understand, then I cannot help you out, and you must wait until you unfold in understanding. But I would say that a re-reading of both this work and "Mental Magic" is advisable—several re-readings, in fact. *Each time that you re-read it you will find something new that you had previously overlooked,* and each reading will discover *many hidden meanings now suddenly made plain.*

ESSENTIALS OF SUCCESS.

The man who wishes to be successful in his dealings with his fellow-men must surround himself with a Positive Mental Atmosphere. He must create an atmosphere of Self-Reliance and Positivity that will overcome the Negativity of those with whom he comes in contact. This Positive Mental Atmosphere is that subtle influence that emanates from the strong men of affairs, and which affects, influences and controls people to a greater degree than the flow of words which many affect, believing it to be the key of success. When you come in contact with one having a Mental Atmosphere of this kind you are affected by it, consciously and unconsciously. And if it has this effect on you in the case of other persons, why should you not reach out and possess this power yourself? Why should you not be a Positive instead of a Negative?

HOW TO PROCEED.

The directions and exercises given in this chapter, coupled with the instruction given in other chapters of the book, should enable you to develop around yourself a most Positive Mental Atmosphere, that will make you a Power. But it all depends upon yourself—you must exercise your Will and Desire, just as you would a muscle that you wished to develop. The same rule operates in the mental as well as in the physical world. In addition to the Exercises given a little further back I would suggest that the following may prove useful to some of you, in special cases, in forming the Positive Mental Atmosphere. I will merely give you the verbal framework, and you must build around it the Mental Picture, which in turn produces the Mental Atmosphere. But, remember, even in practicing these exercises never lose sight of the Main Statement of Strength: "I AM A LIVING ELECTRO-MAGNET," for that Statement will impart Life, Vitality and Energy to the other Mental Images and Statements.

Here are the Statements referred to—the Verbal Framework around which you are to build your Mental Picture that you wish to Materialize on the objective plane. You will find them useful in many cases:

MENTAL FRAMEWORKS.

I. I Surround Myself with an Atmosphere of Success.

II. I am Positive. I have a Strong Will. I make a Positive Impression on those coming into my Field of Force.

III. I Am FEARLESS—Absolutely Fearless—Nothing can Harm Me.

IV. I Kill Out All Worry and Discouragement—I Radiate Hope, Cheerfulness and Good Nature. I

Am Bright, Cheerful and Happy, and make all around me feel the same way.

V. I am Well Poised, Calm and Self-Controlled. I have a perfect Mastery over my Temper, Emotions and Passions, and All recognize this to be a fact.

VII. I am at Ease here, and all Bashfulness and Timidity has departed. I am Calm, at Ease and feel at Home.

VIII. People like me—I am surrounded with a Mental Atmosphere that causes People to Like Me.

IX. I am Master of my surroundings—nothing disturbs—nothing affects me adversely—I am Master.

X. I am surrounded with a Mental Atmosphere of Protection. No one's adverse thoughts, currents or suggestions can penetrate this Protective Armor. I am safe from mental attacks. I am Safe, Strong and Positive.

In using any of the above Statements be sure to follow my advice and instructions regarding the Mental Images, etc., which *put flesh on these verbal skeletons and make a Living Force out of these dry-bony words.* Remember the importance of Mental Imaging and Visualization in this matter of creating Mental Atmospheres.

CHAPTER XVII.

DIRECT PERSONAL INFLUENCE.

In the last chapter I spoke of the effect of Mental Atmospheres with which people may and do surround themselves. You will notice that in my discussion of that part of the subject I spoke only of the *general influence* exerted upon others, and not of the Direct Personal Influence exerted by one man upon another in personal intercourse. The present chapter, and those following it, shall be devoted to the part of the subject just referred to—the Direct Personal Influence.

THE SILENT MENTAL CONFLICT.

As I have told you elsewhere, every time two people meet there ensues a silent mental conflict, or struggle for supremacy, from which one or the other emerges a victor, and which victory is fully recognized by both of the parties to the proceeding. This mental struggle is usually the combat between the general mental powers of the two, without regard to special mental states induced at the time. But, the man who is skilled in the art of Mental Fascination goes further than this, for he recognizes that he may concentrate his Mentative Energy into definite shape and form, and focus the force of his Mental Imagery direct upon the other person, with such force and power that the second person will have a similar mental state induced in him, along the lines familiar to the students of this book.

THE LINES OF OPERATION.

This Direct Personal Influence operates along the lines of both Desire Force and Will Power, of course. I have explained elsewhere how the Will Power may be used to awaken Desire in another; and how it may also capture the Will of the second person. I have also explained how Desire-Force induces a similar Desire in the second person; and also how it is often used to captivate the Will of the other person. It is not necessary for me to repeat these things—you are supposed to be fully acquainted with them, from your study of this book and "Mental Magic." And so I shall proceed to a consideration of the Instruments of Expression of Personal Influence, and the methods usually employed by those using it.

THE INSTRUMENTS OF EXPRESSION.

These instruments of Expression may be classified as follows:

1. Suggestive Instruments, consisting of (a) The Suggestive Manner, and (b) The Suggestive Tone, and (c) The Suggestive Word,

2. The Instrument of the Eye;

3. The Instrument of the Touch;

and all of these three forms are, of course, merely the Instruments by which, and through which, the Mind expresses itself—the channel through which pours the Mentative Energy. Let us consider them in the above order.

SUGGESTIVE INSTRUMENTS.

I will ask you now to turn to my chapter on "Mental Suggestion," in my work on "Mental Magic." You will see therein stated the active principles of Mental Suggestion, with which you should thoroughly familiarize yourself, for I shall not repeat the instructions in this book. You will see there that Suggestion is the outward symbol of the inward Mental State, and that it is the inner state that gives vitality to the Suggestion. Get this idea fixed firmly in your mind, and always think of the Force behind the Suggestion. I have explained to you, also, that when one receives a Suggestion through a Physical agent, he has induced in himself the mental state corresponding to the one originating that Physical Suggestion. For example, if you feel yourself filled with Confidence, Energy and Fearlessness, your outward appearance will *reflect* that inner state, and the outer appearance will become a Suggestion to others. These others will instinctively feel that your inner state is as I have stated. And, this being so, a Physical Suggestion made stronger than usual will produce a deeper impression on others than would any ordinary suggestion.

THE SUGGESTIVE MANNER.

In view of the above, you will see why it is that those familiar with the subject deem it important to cultivate the Suggestive Instruments. Beginning with (a) the Suggestive Manner, you will see why it is that we are impressed with the manner of a man who manifests Energy, Self-Confidence, and Power in every motion. And also, why we have confidence in a man whose manner indicates that he is a person used to being trusted by others—accustomed to having confidence reposed in him. And so I might mention hundreds of examples tending to show that if a man's manner conveys the impression that he is used to being treated in a certain way, and that he is accustomed to acting in a certain way, we are very apt to accept the Suggestion of Manner, and fall into line with the rest of people. And if the man happens to be a good actor, we may be imposed upon and fooled by his Suggestive Manner.

THE RULE WORKS BOTH WAYS.

Not only does this law hold good in the case of the manner and appearance of Success, Strength, Confidence, etc., but it also operates along the lines of the appearance and manner of Failure, Weakness, and Distrust. Do you not know of cases wherein you have felt that certain persons were not worthy of Confidence; or were not to be depended upon where Strength of Character was required; or were not likely to Succeed? Of course you have, and you acted upon the Suggestion, too.

AN ILLUSTRATION.

In illustrating this point, I have frequently used the illustration of the two dogs, the one carrying himself in a manner betokening Self-Respect and an ability to prevent and resent undue liberties, and the other carrying his tail between his legs, in a manner and appearance indicating that he expected to be kicked and cuffed. The first dog is almost invariably treated with respect, even by the most mischievous youngsters; while the second one almost always invites to himself the kicks, tin cans and brick bats of the young hoodlums of the neighborhood. And this illustration is as true in the case of people as in the case of dogs. Better take the hint!

HOW TO ACQUIRE THIS MANNER.

But, you may say, how is one to acquire the proper Suggestive Manner? My answer is that there is but one sure way, and that is to begin to Think Out the Park; Visualize it; and Act it Out. You will see the philosophy of this in my lesson on "Mental Architecture," in my work on "Mental Magic." In other words, if you wish to convey a Suggestive Manner of Confidence, you must begin to THINK "Confidence" from morning until night. And you must also begin to Visualize "Confidence" when you have the chance to do so—that is, you must make a Mental Picture of yourself as manifesting Confidence. And you must also begin to ACT OUT THE PART.

ACTING OUT YOUR PART.

Now about this Acting Out, I would say that I mean not only the "playing the part" in your interviews with people, but I also mean an *actual series of rehearsals* in private, just as you would do if you were preparing to play a part on the stage, in public. You must form a Mental Image of how you would look and act if you were filled with Confidence, and were approaching people. You will find that practice will improve you very much in this way, and that you will soon acquire a manner that will be like second-nature, and will really serve to give the Suggestion of your

Manner to others with whom you come in contact. And, more than this, it will actually tend to build up confidence in yourself. Imagine yourself as approaching strange people, and then act out the part the best you know how, improving a little in ease, and smoothness of action each day. Think of how the actor on the stage impresses you—and then remember that the manner was acquired by constant practice, and work. And you may do the same, and may manage to impress other people just as the actor does you. And what is true in the case of "Confidence" is true regarding any Character that you wish to play. Any and all Characters may be played out in this way, and an appearance and manner acquired which will give the Suggestion to others. I wish I could make you realize how much there is in this method. If you could realize how some men have used it to acquire qualities that have enabled them to prey upon the public, you would realize how important it might be for you for legitimate and honorable use.

PRACTICE MAKES PERFECT.

In this Acting Out, you must remember that the practice will make you so perfect that the part will appear natural when you play it in public. But without practice, an attempt to play it in public will make one ridiculous. Remember the illustration of the real actor, and you will have the secret of Acting Out.

And also remember this, that in the measure that you "throw your mind" into the part, so will be your success. When you practice, you must throw your mind into the acting, just as you would if you were in earnest. It is the Mind back of it all, remember.

THE SUGGESTIVE TONE.

The second Suggestive Instrument is the Suggestive Tone. This, too, may be acquired by Acting Out. You must practice until you are able to express your meaning with "feeling" that all who hear may be impressed. You should begin your practice by choosing some simple words in every-day use—"Good Morning!" for instance. Try it now, and see how roughly, clumsily and crudely you give the morning greeting. Then try to imagine that you are full of good cheer, energy, and brightness, and then throw your feeling into your "good morning," and see how different it seems. Practice this awhile and you will soon acquire a natural, cheery, bright, and invigorating tone when you say "good morning." You will not need a teacher in elocution to tell you how to do this. Try to FEEL the part, and you will express it naturally. Make your Feelings more flexible, and your Tones will reflect them. After you have mastered the simpler terms of expression, work up to larger sentences, and speeches. Try them on the chairs in your room, in imagining that people are seated therein; speak to them feelingly and with expression, until you acquire the art. You will not realize how much you may gain by such practice, until you actually try it. I wish that you could hear the testimony of some people to whom I have taught this thing.

THE IMPORTANCE OF IT.

There is nothing more important in Personal Influence than a good Suggestive Tone. Think of the people that you know, and then remember what an influence their voices have on you. Not only the quality of the voice, but the *Tone*. You readily recognize the difference between the tone of the hesitating, timid, self-doubting person, and that of the confident, self-reliant individual. There is a subtle vibration about the tone of the latter that causes one to feel confidence and respect, and which exacts obedience in a quiet, calm way, devoid of bluster or rant. Read what I have said on this subject, in my lesson on "Personal Influence" in my work on "Mental Magic."

EXAMPLES OF ITS USE.

If you will read the part of the present book dealing with Psychological Experimentation, you will see that much depends upon the Tone. You will see that when you say to a subject, "You CAN'T," the tone in which you say "CAN'T" goes a long way toward producing the response. And so it is with the Suggestive Tone, no matter what it is made to express. It always impresses upon one that the speaker using it *means what he says.* And that is why many public men practice year after year in mastering this Instrument of Influence—the Suggestive Tone. Again would I refer you to the example of the Actor—see how he manages to throw FEELING into his Tone. And you may do likewise, if you will but practice in earnest, and *throw your mind into the work.* Think of the thing you wish to express—visualize it—and then act it out in your Tone. You will be surprised at the rapid progress that you will make. Remember always, though, the Tone is but the Instrument of Expression of the MIND back of it.

USE NERVES, NOT MUSCLES.

Many people make the mistake of "speaking with the muscles instead of with their nerves," as one writer has expressed it. In other words, they seem to throw *muscular force* into their tones, instead of *nervous energy*, and in so doing they make a great mistake, for the former has a dull, non-penetrating effect, whereas the latter vibrates subtly and reaches the feeling part of one's mind. FEEL, FEEL, FEEL, when you wish to speak impressively, and your Tones will reflect the same, and induce a corresponding feeling in others.

THE SUGGESTIVE WORD.

The Third Form of the Suggestive Instrument is The Suggestive Word. I may be able to explain this more clearly when I call your attention to the fact that EACH WORD IS A CRYSTALLIZED THOUGHT. In every word there is an imprisoned Thought. And when you lodge a Word in the mind of another person, the crystal covering is dissolved, and the released thought manifests itself. And, this being so, it becomes important for one to carefully choose the crystallized thoughts, or words, which he wishes to implant in the mind of another. I have spoken of this in my larger work, in my lesson on "Mental Suggestion," to which I refer you. But I wish here to say to you, again, that you should study words until you are able to distinguish between those which carry a *live, active, feeling* thought, and those less strong.

EXAMPLES.

Take the word "STRONG," for instance. Does it not make you feel Strength when you hear it forcibly and feelingly pronounced? Take the word "KIND," and see what feelings it arouses in you. Pronounce the words "LION" and "LAMB," and see the different feelings you experience from the differing sounds. Take the word "CRASH," and see how it suggests the crashing, crunching, tearing, startling thing for which it stands. Compare the sound of the words "ROUGH" and "SMOOTH"—and you will see what I mean. The only way that I can point out to you to acquire the use of Suggestive Words is to study Words themselves. Listen to the words used by others, and note their effect on you. Take a small dictionary and run over its pages, and you will soon have a collection of good, strong, effective terms for handy use when occasion demands. A man does not have to be "highly educated" in the usual sense of that term, in order to use Strong Suggestive Words. Some instinctively choose vital words, charged with feeling, and such make their words *felt*. Think over this matter.

NUTSHELL INSTRUCTIONS.

In the use of all the three Suggestive Instruments, remember that the object is to make others FEEL the Mental State you are expressing. That is the whole thing in a nutshell.

CHAPTER XVIII.

EYE-EXPRESSION.

Next in order in our list of Instruments of Mentative Expression is The Eye, that most wonderful of all the human organs, and which is as much an instrument for the Expression of Mentative Force as it is an instrument for receiving the sense-impression of Sight. Let us consider it in its former aspect.

THE EYE AS A SUGGESTIVE INSTRUMENT.

In the first place, the Eye is one of the most potent and effective instruments of Suggestion, although I have not included it in that class. The expression of the eye will induce mental conditions in others along the lines of Suggestion, and those who understand and have mastered this art of using the eyes have at their disposal a wonderful instrument of Suggestive Influence. Those of us who have ever met a very "magnetic" man, or a "charming and fascinating" woman, have carried away with us a lively recollection of "the expression of the eyes" of such a person. Actors and public speakers, as well as those whose business it is to meet and impress people, often make a close study of eye-expression in order to produce a heightened effect along these lines. While this phase of the subject belongs more properly to the various "Schools of Expression" in various parts of the country, it may be worth while to pause a moment and examine some of the leading principles of this Art of Eye-Expression, considered without reference to the phase of Mentative Energy.

EXERCISES IN EYE-EXPRESSION.

Begin by studying your eyes in a mirror. You will see that in the center of the eyeball there is a black spot; this is called the "Pupil" of the eye. The larger circle surrounding the Pupil is called the "Iris." The white of the eye surrounds the Iris. The upper eyelid moving over the eyeball produces a variety of expressions, each giving to the face a totally different appearance, expression of suggestive meaning. We all recognize the meaning of these different expressions, but very few of us understand the mechanism producing the expression. Standing before your mirror, study these various expressions. The following exercises may help you.

EYELID EXERCISES.

1. Hold the upper lid in such a position that its

edge rests half-way between the pupil and top of the iris. This gives an expression of Calmness.

2. Rest the edge of the upper eyelid at the top of the pupil. This gives an expression of Indifference.

3. The edge of the eyelid resting at the top of the iris gives an expression of Strong Interest.

4. The edge of the eyelid resting half-way over the pupil gives an expression of Deep Thought.

5. The edge of the eyelid resting just above the edge of the iris, and thus showing a narrow strip of white between the edge of the lid and the edge of the iris, gives an expression of Emotional Activity.

6. The above position, exaggerated so as to show as much of the white as possible between the edge of the iris and the edge of the lid, will give an expression of Emotional Excitement.

HOW TO PRACTICE THE EXERCISES.

Teachers of the Art of Expression instruct their pupils to practice the above expressions and positions. They find that with a little practice nearly every one may easily acquire the art of expression in the first four exercises, but that the last two are more difficult of acquirement. The last exercise—Emotional Excitement—especially is found to be quite difficult of attainment, and teachers claim that but a small percentage are able to produce the expression without considerable practice. Practice these movements until you can reproduce them without the aid of the mirror, just as a man may learn to shave without a mirror, by constant practice before one. The exercises will not only enable you to express the different mental states easily and freely, but will also tend to strengthen the muscles and nerves of the eyes themselves, providing that you proceed gradually and do not overtask the eyes at the beginning. Do not scowl, or contract the brows in the practices. A few minutes at a time is all that you should use in practicing.

THE SEVENTH EXERCISE.

When you have mastered the above exercises, especially Nos. 5 and 6, you may try the following, which is the most difficult of all:

7. Rest the eyelid in the position of Strong Interest (No. 3), and then *at the same time* lift the edge of the *under lid* to the lower edge of the pupil. This position gives the expression of Close Scrutiny.

THE POWER OF EXPRESSION.

You will be surprised at the added Power of Expression that the careful practice of the above exercises will give you. You will be able to manifest more Suggestive Feeling, and will induce Emotional States of Feeling in others. A little practice will give you such convincing proof of this that you will not need urging to further perfect yourself in them. The Expressions of Emotional Activity and Emotional Excitement especially will produce a startling result if used on appropriate occasions when you wish to exhibit the appearance of the deepest Emotional Excitement and Force.

DEVELOPMENT EXERCISES.

The following Development Exercises are highly recommended by teachers who have devoted years of study and practice along these lines:

1. Open the eyes quite widely, but not so widely as to strain them, and hold them in that position for a few seconds, gazing into your mirror, which must be directly in front of you on a level with your eyes. While gazing open them a trifle wider still, without straining, and throw an intense expression into them. Do not move the eyebrows, but allow them to remain normal.

2. Resume the above position, and then change to the expression of Strong Interest (see previous exercises), looking at yourself in the glass just as you would in looking at another person with that expression.

3. Resume position 1, and then gradually change to the expression of Emotional Activity (see previous exercises), gazing at yourself in the mirror.

4. Resume position 1, and then gradually change to the expression of Emotional Excitement (see previous exercises) gazing at yourself in the mirror.

5. Resume position 1, and then gradually change to the expression of Close Scrutiny (see previous exercises), gazing at yourself in the mirror.

In the above exercises you must act as if the reflection of yourself in the mirror were in reality another person whom you wished to influence. The better you act this out, the better will your results be.

6. Practice the expression of Strong Interest on persons to whom you are listening, until you feel that you have awakened a response in them. I may add that the expression of DEEP INTEREST consists of but the same expression heightened by *more feeling* behind it; and the expression of LOVING INTEREST is the same, "only more so." This "more feeling" may be either real or assumed, as in the case of the good actor.

7. Practice the expression of Close Scrutiny upon other persons upon appropriate occasions in which you desire to appear as taking a deep, critical interest in some proposition, undertaking, theory, etc. Many persons have built up a reputation for being "good listeners" and "keen observers" by this practice. I mention it for what it may be worth to you. I am merely giving you the "rules of the game," not necessarily advising you to play it.

CHAPTER XIX.

THE FASCINATION OF THE EYE.

And now I have reached that part of my subject in which I must speak of the *Power of the Eye to convey Mentative Force.* Owing to some law of nervous mechanism not fully understood as yet, the eye is one of the most effective mediums for the passage of Mentative Currents from one person to another. I shall not attempt to indulge in any special theory on the subject, but shall proceed to the description of the facts of the case. I may add, however, that advanced occultists inform us that portions of the human brain, during a manifestation of strong emotional effort, or exercise of Will, resembles an incandescent surface, glowing and phosphorescent. And that also there are seen great beams of this incandescent energy streaming out from the eyes of the person, and reaching the mind of other persons. And more than this, these "beams" of energy transmit mental states, thoughts, etc., of the person, just as scientists have found that "beams of light" will carry waves of electricity, and have thus been able to send telegraphic, and even telephonic messages over such beams of light.

MENTATIVE BEAMS OF ENERGY.

One who has mastered the Fascination of the Eye, is able to convey most readily to others the Mentative Currents which tend to produce similar mental states by Mentative Induction, as explained elsewhere in this book, and in "Mental Magic." If you will but remember the above illustration of the "beam of light" along which the electric and magnetic currents travel, and will form a Mental Picture of these Mentative Beams from the Eye, you will understand the process much better, and you will at the same time tend to give to your own Mentative beams a substantial reality, along the lines of Visualization. That is, when you wish to use these Mentative Beams, you should *imagine* them as actually existing in full force and reality—this will tend to cause to give them a material reality, and thus render them a highly efficient medium for the passage of your Mentative Currents.

THE FASCINATING GAZE.

And now, right here is the best place to instruct you in the proper use of the eye in what has been called "The Magnetic Gaze," but which would be more properly styled the "Fascinating Gaze." There has been much nonsense written on this subject, and in some of my own earlier writings I gave directions along these lines which I am now able to replace with more approved methods, and later discoveries coming from the study and experimentation of myself and others along these lines. I am willing to improve upon my own methods as well as upon those of others—I have no false pride upon this subject, and if tomorrow I find that I can improve upon my work of today, I will do so and give my students the benefit of the change, instead of stubbornly "sticking to it," just because I had once stated a theory, fact, or result. There is no standing still in scientific work—he who stands still really goes backward.

THE FORMER METHOD.

The former instructions regarding the "Magnetic Gaze" told the student to concentrate his gaze "at the root of the nose" of the other person, that is, right between his two eyes. Now this was all very well, but there is a far better plan. This focusing the gaze between the eyes of the other person, really results in "crossing" your gaze, and thus robbing it of a portion of the direct electro-magnetic power that it possesses. You may prove this by holding up a pencil before your eyes, and focusing your eyes upon it as you draw it nearer and nearer to your eyes. The nearer you get to the pencil, or to the other person, the more will your gaze be "crossed" and the effect impaired. A gaze from a pair of "crossed eyes" is not nearly so Fascinating as one from a pair of straight eyes, giving out a direct, forceful impression.

THE NEW METHOD.

The new "Fascinating Gaze" is performed as follows: You *do not* focus your gaze at a point between the two eyes of the other person, but, instead, you gaze directly and straightly into his two eyes with your two eyes. You will find this difficult, and tiring, if you perform it in the ordinary way—and herein lies the "secret." Instead of focusing your eyes upon his, as if you really wished to *see* the color of his eyes, you must so focus your eyes that you are really gazing *through him,* as if he were transparent and you wished to *see something beyond him.* A little practice before a mirror will show you what I mean better than I can explain it to you in words. Practice at "*gazing through*" objects will aid you in acquiring this gaze. Try for instance focusing your eyes upon the wall opposite you as you raise your eyes from this page. Then as you look at the wall, slowly pass your hand before your eyes at a distance of about two feet, but don't change your focus—*don't see the hand plainly,* but keep your gaze focused on the wall, *as if you could see it through the hand.*

HOW TO PRACTICE.

This gaze must not consist of a blank, vacant, stupid state, but must be intense and earnest. Practice on objects as above stated, and with your mirror, will aid you in perfecting the gaze. It will help you if you have some friend with whom you can practice it.

THE EFFECT UPON OTHERS.

The other person will not be aware that you are not "seeing" him, and are "*gazing through*" him—to him it will appear that you are giving him a very deep, intense, steady, earnest glance. He will see your pupils dilate, as they always do when looking at a distant object, and your expression will be one of calm, serene power.

IT DOES NOT TIRE THE EYES.

And another important point about this gaze is that you may maintain it a long time without tiring the eyes, and without the eyes watering or blinking. You may out-stare another person, or animal, in this way, without fatigue, while the other's eyes grow tired and weak. So much is this true that the results of my own investigation of the subject have convinced me that the animals who manifest the Fascinating Gaze (as mentioned in a previous chapter) really focus their eyes beyond the object in just this way. If ever you get a chance to observe an animal fascinating another, you will see that I am right in this theory.

THE SCIENTIFIC EXPLANATION.

This "*gazing through*" the other person is accomplished by a certain "accommodation" of the eye, as oculists and opticians call it, and while you are performing it you cannot examine distinctly, or "see" distinctly the eyes of the other person, because your focus is different. To show you why you are able to maintain this gaze such a long time without tiring your eyes, I would remind you of the ease with which you may maintain the expression of being "wrapped in thought," "day-dreaming," "lost in a brown study," "just thinking about things," etc., with which you all are familiar. In such a mental state you are able to "gaze into space" for a long time without the slightest fatigue, while a few seconds' focusing your eyes upon a near-by object will tire them very much indeed. And then, again, you know how long you are able to gaze at an object far out at sea, or far across the desert, or far down or across the mountain, without tiring your eyes. The whole secret is that short-range focusing upon an object tires the eyes much more than does "long-range" gazing into space. This being the case, it will tire you far less "seeing through" a person, than gazing at him and "seeing" him at short range.

RULES FOR PRACTICE.

In practicing the maintaining of the gaze for a long time, I would advise against tiring the eyes by gazing at short-range objects. Better practice at gazing at distant objects until you are able to maintain the gaze a long time, as you will be able to do after a little practice. In fact, I advise you to practice the "gazing into space," because proficiency in that will enable you to perfect the Fascinating Gaze. After you have practiced this "*gazing through*" method a bit, you will be able to look at an object a couple of feet away, and gaze right through it—that is, you will not consciously "see" it objectively, although apparently staring hard at it.

MAKE HASTE SLOWLY.

Avoid all exercises tiring to the eyes, and proceed slowly, working from trifling successes to more important ones. You will be surprised how a little intelligent practice along these lines will give you a penetrating glance, firm, earnest, and full of "magnetism" and Fascination, without the slightest sense of strain, fatigue or effort. You have long wished for such an expression—here it is for you.

CHAPTER XX.

THE USE OF THE MENTATIVE INSTRUMENTS.

In the use of the Eyes for the purpose of conveying Mentative Currents, you should always remember that the FEELING is the real power behind these currents of Force, and that the Brain is the Dynamo from which the currents originate. The Brain, you know, is the great Transformer, or Converter of the Mentative Energy, and acts just as does a Dynamo in the direction of sending forth great waves of Force. Consequently, if you wish to send out Mentative Currents for the purpose of inducing feeling in others, you must first have FEELING generated in your Mental Dynamo.

VALUABLE EXERCISES.

It will be well for two people to practice the Eye Exercises together, but in the absence of a friend in whom you have confidence, you may obtain excellent results by practicing before your friendly mirror. In either case, you must first arouse in your mind the

Feeling that you wish to express in Mentative Currents. Put your Feeling into your glance, and it will be felt.

Exercise 1. Look into the eyes of your friend (or your own in the mirror) and then say *mentally* "I am Stronger than you." Throw into your glance as much of the feeling of Strength as you can.

Exercise 2. Say *mentally*, "I am more Positive than you—I am outgazing you," throwing as much positivity as possible into your gaze, the same being inspired, of course, by your Feeling.

Exercise 3. Say, and *feel*, "You are afraid of me —I am making you feel my Strength," throwing the feeling into your gaze.

ACTUAL PRACTICE.

After you have acquired the faculty of making your strength felt by the above exercises you may use same upon other people when the occasion renders it advisable. If you are addressed by some person whom you think is trying to master you mentatively, or whose strong influence you wish to ward off, you may use the above method on him. As a rule the person who is doing the talking has a slight advantage over the listener, all else being equal. The speaker is the more positive because he is expressing more Energy. But you may counteract this, if you are the listener, by simply sending him a glance, accompanied by the

Feeling of "*I scatter your Force into bits—you cannot affect ME!*"

POINTS OF PRACTICE.

In resisting an attack of this sort, keep your mouth closed, with the teeth touching, for this "bite" denotes Strength and Firmness, and brings into play the parts of the brain manifesting these qualities, and thus charges your Mentative Currents with these feelings. At the same time gaze firmly and steadily into the eyes of the other, using the Fascinating Gaze. I would bid you remember my remarks in "Mental Magic" about the person *standing* having the advantage of the one *sitting*. Avoid the sitting position when the other person is standing—do not give him this advantage, but take it yourself if you can.

MENTAL COMMANDS AND REFUSALS.

In speaking to persons and requesting them to do something, you should accompany the verbal request by a Mental Command. For instance, if you say "You will do this for me, *won't* you?" (this is the Suggestive Form of Questioning, remember) you should accompany the question with the COMMAND (made mentally) with the proper glance, "You WILL do this." If you are the person requested to do something that you do not wish to do, you should answer, "No, I do not care to do this," or "I do not see my way clear to do it," or "I am unable to oblige you," etc., etc., but at the same time you must send the *mental answer,* with its accompanying glance, "I WILL NOT do it, and you cannot *make* me."

CERTAIN DANGEROUS TEACHING.

A well-known teacher along these lines several years ago, taught his pupils to gaze into the eyes of persons whom they wished to affect, at the same time saying mentally: "*I am looking at you. I am looking through your eyes into your brain. My will power is stronger than yours. You are under my control. I will compel you to do what I wish. You must do what I say. You shall do this. Do it at once.*" It will readily be seen that this will generate a powerful Mentative Current, if there is a sufficiently strong Feeling—Will and Desire—behind it. But right here I shall give you *an Antidote for this kind of Influence.* In all cases where you are attacked mentally in this way you may dissolve the Force by a POSITIVE DENIAL.

THE POSITIVE DENIAL.

The POSITIVE DENIAL is the powerful Force that scatters into tiny bits the Force directed against one. It is *a destructive agent,* just as is the POSITIVE STATEMENT a constructive or creative one.

One who understands the scientific use of this destructive force may undo the mentative work of others, to a surprising degree. Some day I shall have more to say regarding these two warring forces, along the broader lines of the entire subject of Telementation, but at present I shall confine myself to their use in Personal Influence. *By a Strong, Positive Denial, You may scatter and disintegrate any Mentative Influence directed against you.* This formula will give you a general idea of it. Suppose that you are repelling a Statement such as given above. In that case you should say *mentally*, accompanying it with the proper glance, with Feeling back of it: "I DENY POSITIVELY your power over Me. *I Deny it out of existence.* I WILL NOT do your bidding, and I DENY your right and Power to command me. I DENY *your* power, and I affirm *my own.*"

HOW TO CULTIVATE THIS POWER.

You may cultivate this power to use the POSITIVE DENIAL by practicing on an imaginary person whom you may suppose is trying to influence you. Imagine the strong, positive person before you, trying to influence you and then start in to practice the Positive Denial on him, until you feel that you have beaten him off, and have sent him flying away in retreat. These imaginary mental battles will develop a great power of mentative resistance in you, and I advise you strengthen yourselves along these lines, if you feel that you are weak. You may improve on the above exercise, by imagining that after your enemy is in full retreat you follow him up and pour Statement after Statement into him, changing your position from a defender into an attacking force.

MENTATIVE FENCING LESSONS.

These imaginary rehearsals will do more for one than people think possible. They are like stage rehearsals that make perfect the actors. They are the fencing lessons from which the swordsman gains skill, and strength. Practice, *practice,* PRACTICE makes perfect in everything—in Mentative work as well as physical. There are good psychological and occult reasons behind this method and practice, but I shall not enter upon that field at present—this book is intended to give you the "how" of the subject, rather than the "why."

THE SECRET OF EFFECTIVE SPEAKING.

In personal conversation with another you will find it of the greatest value to see as clearly as possible a mental picture, chart or map, of what you are saying to him. By so doing you will impress most forcibly upon his mind that which you wish him to see, and feel. In this statement is compressed the Secret of Effective Speaking. In the degree that YOU see and feel the thought that you are expressing in words, will be the degree of Impression made upon, and Mentative Induction produced in, the other person. The secret of course lies in the Law of Visualization as explained in "Mental Magic" and in this book.

PSYCHOLOGICAL EXPERIMENTS.

You may find an evidence of your increasing Mentative Influence by trying the psychological experiment of "Willing" people to move this way or that way, by gazing intently at them. In this experiment it is not necessary for you to gaze into their eyes. Gazing at their back, preferably at the upper part of the neck, at the base of the brain, will answer. You may try "willing" persons to look around on the street, or in public places, etc. Or you may "will" that they turn to the right or left of you, when approaching each other on the street. Or, in stores you may "will" that a certain clerk, from out of a number, will step forward to wait upon you. These and many similar experiments have an interest to the majority of students, and are accomplished with comparative ease, after sufficient practice. The whole theory and practice consists of a steady gaze, and the *Mental command,* and will, that the person will act so-and-so, together with the *earnest expectation* that they will obey the command, and the *mental picture* of their doing so. That is all there is to it.

GENERAL ADVICE.

In the use of the Eye as a Mentative Instrument, remember first, last, and all the time, that DESIRE and WILL are the phases of the Mentative Energy, and that in the degree that Desire is kindled, and Will is exerted, so will be the Power expressed by yourself, and impressed upon others. Read "Mental Magic" over a number of times, until you have fully grasped the underlying principles. Then re-read the present book, and commit its exercises and instructions to memory. Then practice frequently, and perfect yourself in the methods pointed out, until you render them "second nature." You will be conscious of a gradual growth and development, along the lines of Mentative Power and Influence. The flame of Electro-Magnetic Power once lit will never die out—tend the flame carefully, keep the wick trimmed clean, and fill the lamp with oil, and it will ever burn bright and emit heat and light and Power.

THE MAGNETIC TOUCH.

The last Mentative Instrument mentioned in a previous chapter is the Touch. There was a time, in my early stages of experimentation and psychological research, when I laughed at the idea of the Touch playing any real part in the work of Mental Influence. Of course I saw the effect of the Touch in certain phases of psychological work, but I believed that it was all "merely suggestion," but I soon learned that the Touch was really a most potent Instrument of Mentative Energy. I now explain it by the idea of the nerves being like the wires upon which the electric current travels. The Brain is the Dynamo, or Converter of the Energy, and while the latter travels in waves and currents without any wires (just as does the wave of the wireless telegraph) still *if there is a wire to be had,* then it follows the lines of least resistance and takes advantage of the nerve-wire. Certain parts of the body have nerve-cells very highly developed in them—are in fact miniature brains. In the cases of some persons of sensitive and trained touch, there exist little clusters of nerve cells at the ends of the fingers, that act like miniature brains. The lips are also highly developed in this respect, as the well known phenomena of "kissing" evidences. The fingers and hand are excellent polar mediums for conveying the Mentative Energy that pours down over the nerves from the Brain, and through which it passes to the other person.

HOW TO USE THE HANDS.

The use of the Touch of the hands as a channel for conveying Mentative Energy depends greatly upon the development of the hands by the individual. Those who understand this matter, develop the conductivity of the hands by "treating" them, as follows: Think of your hands as excellent conductors of Mentative Energy, and imagine that you can feel the Energy pouring down the nerves of your arms, and out of your hands, obeying your Will, when you shake hands with people. You will soon develop your hands to such a degree that some sensitive persons will actually "feel" the current passing into them. Always accompany the passage of the current with the thought or feeling that you wish to induce in the other person, just as you do when you use the Fascinating Gaze. In fact, the Gaze and the hand clasp should be used together, when possible, for by so doing you double the effect.

THE MAGNETIC HAND-CLASP.

When you shake hands with a person *throw Mind and Feeling into it,* and do not fall into the mechanical, lifeles method so common among people. Throw your Feeling down to your hand, and at the same time make a mental command or statement appropriate to the case. For instance, grasp the person's hand with Feeling, and interest, saying, mentally, at the same time: *"You Like Me."* Then, when you draw your hand away, if possible let your fingers slide over the palm of his hand in a caressing manner, allowing his first finger to pass between your thumb and forefinger, close up in the crotch of the thumb. Practice this well, until you can perform it without thinking of it—

that is, make it your natural way of shaking hands. You will find that this method of shaking hands will open up a new interest in people toward you, and in other ways you will discover its advantage. You never knew a "fascinating" person who did not have a good hand-clasp. It is a part of the fascinating personality.

OTHER USES OF THE HANDS.

There are many persons, well grounded on the psychological principles underlying Mental Fascination, who use the hands as a medium for Mentative Energy, without shaking hands. For instance, they sit near the other person and place their hands so that their fingers will point toward him, at the same time *willing* that the current flow through the fingers and toward the other. They also use their hands in conversation so as to have the tips of their fingers pointing toward the other. This last plan becomes highly effective when used with the appropriate gestures, for it is akin to the mesmeric "pass" of the hands. In this connection I would say beware of the person who is always trying to put his hands on you—beware of the "pawing over" process. Avoid it in the ordinary way, if possible, or else deliberately practice the POSITIVE DENIAL toward the person, holding the idea and mental statement that "I DENY the power of your magnetism—I scatter it by my Denial."

A WARNING TO WOMEN.

In concluding this chapter, I would especially caution young women and older ones, for that matter, against allowing men to be familiar with them in the direction of "holding hands," or similar practices. Not only does this "familiarity breed contempt" but there are good psychological reasons why the practice is to be condemned. You have seen what part the hands play in "magnetizing" as it is called, and is it not clearly discernible how one may use the hands in this "petting," and all that sort of thing, in order to psychologically affect another person? I am not speaking now of the caresses indulged in by honorable true lovers—for all the talk in the world would not change that sort of thing—but I am alluding to the indiscriminate "pawing over" on the part of strange men that some young girls allow. There is a danger in this sort of thing, and I want you to know it. If you have daughters, or young female relatives, warn them against this thing, and *tell them the reason why.*

A CAUTION TO MEN.

And the same thing is true of the man who is always patting other men on the shoulder, or resting his arm around them, or else "taking hold of them" in a friendly caressing way during a conversation. Such men may not know the psychology of the thing, but they have found out that this sort of "patting up" makes other men more impressible, and amenable to their influence, and so they practice it. Make them stop it, either by moving away, or by POSITIVE DENIAL.

THE PROTECTIVE ARMOR.

Now, once more, remember the power of this POSITIVE DENIAL as a disperser, and disintegrator of Adverse Influence. If this book taught you nothing else, it would still be "worth while" to you because of this one point of instruction. For this Positive Denial is a Mentative Armor that will protect you—a Mentative Sword that will defend you—a Mentative Lightning Flash that will clear the Mental Atmosphere. Learn the Secret of Positive Statement, and Positive Denial, and you are clad in an invulnerable armor and are armed with the weapon of Strength—and so you may, like the "Warrior Bold" go "gaily to the fray." May the Victory be yours!

CHAPTER XXI.

CONCLUDING INSTRUCTION.

We have now reached the end of our consideration of the subject of "Mental Fascination," in this book. But you have reached only the beginning of the subject, when you close these pages, for the real subject rests in the action of the principles in real life.

THE EFFECT OF THE INSTRUCTION.

Though you may not feel disposed to put into operation much of the instruction given herein, yet, from your very acquaintance with what has been taught in these pages, you will be compelled to *see* the operation of the principles in the everyday life around you. You will see them in operation on every side, now that you are familiar with their laws of operation. And you will find yourself instinctively guarding against its influence, just as you would guard against a threatened physical blow. And you will be surprised, and perhaps pained sometimes, at seeing people trying to influence you in this way, whom you would not have suspected of doing so. On the whole, you will be a much stronger man or woman by reason of the information herein given you. And you will have the advantage of knowing how to resist, defeat and dispel the adverse influences that may be used to influence you. Remember the assertion of the Positive Will, and the use of the Positive Denial!

ADDITIONAL INFORMATION.

There is one thing more that I wish to call your attention to, before closing, although, strictly speaking, it forms part of the subject of Telemental Influence rather than that of Mental Fascination. I have mentioned this matter in my work on "Mental Magic," in my lesson on "The Science of Telementation." I allude to the use of Telementation for the purpose of Mental Fascination, which is performed by some persons who have become acquainted with the subject.

DISTANT FASCINATION.

The person wishing to influence another at a distance, just as he would in the case of a Personal Interview, forms a Mental Image of the person whom he wishes to influence, and then proceeds just as if the person was actually before him, according to the methods mentioned in this book. I know of at least one teacher who advises his students to "treat" prospective customers, and others with whom they expect to have dealings, or relations, as follows: "Imagine your prospective customer, or other person, as seated in a chair before which you are standing. Make the imagined picture as strong as possible, for upon this depends your success. Then proceed to 'treat' the person just as you would if he were actually present. Concentrate your will upon him, and tell him just what you expect to tell him when you meet him. Use all of the arguments that you can think of, and at the same time hold the thought that he MUST do as you say. Try to imagine him as complying with your wishes, in every respect, for this imagining will tend to 'come true' when you really meet the person. This rule may be used, not only in the case of prospective customers, but also in the cases of persons whom you wish to *influence in any way whatsoever*."

HOW TO COUNTERACT THE INFLUENCE.

Now, all this is very plain to the student of this book, and of my work on "Mental Magic," for the principles employed are familiar to my students. The result of a practice like the above would undoubtedly tend to clear a "mentative path" in the other person's mind, and make easier the effect of a subsequent interview. For the other person would be thus accustomed to the idea, thought or feeling, and the work of clearing away the mental underbrush would be done in advance. But, fortunately for us all, we have the Antidote for this Bane, if we have acquainted ourselves with the underlying principles of the subject. So important do I regard this matter of Self-Protection against this Telemental Influencing that I purpose adding to my remarks on this subject several paragraphs from my book on "Mental Magic," which, although you have already read them, should appear right in this place, in order to be impressed upon your mind in connection with what I have just said. I want you all to read again what I have said on this subject of Self-Protection. So here is the reproduction of a few rules to use on occasions when you think that someone is trying to so "treat" or "influence you. Better study them carefully. Here they are:

VALUABLE RULES.

1. In the first place, steady your mind, and calm your feelings. Then pause for a moment, and say the words, "I AM," calmly and forcibly, at the same time forming a mental picture of yourself as a Centre of Force and Power in the Great Ocean of Mind. See yourself as standing alone and full of Power. Then mentally form a picture of your Aura, extending about a yard on all sides of you, in an egg-shaped form. See that this Aura is charged with your Will-Power, which is flowing outward repelling any adverse mental suggestions that are being sent to you, and causing them to fly back to the source from whence they came. A little practice will enable you

to perfect this picture, which will greatly aid you in creating a strong Positive Aura of Will, which will prove to be a Magnetic Armor and shield.

A USEFUL AFFIRMATION.

The affirmation "I AM" is the strongest known to Occult Science, for it is a positive statement of Actual Being. You may use the following Affirmation also, if you please—it has helped many: *"I assert my Individuality as a Centre of Force, Power and Being. Nothing can adversely affect me. My Mind is mine own, and I refuse admittance to unwelcome suggestions for influences. My Desires are my own, and refuse to admit undesirable vibrations by Induction or otherwise. My Will is my own, and I charge it with Power to beat off and repel all undesirable influences. I am surrounded by an Aura of Positive Will, which protects me absolutely."*

A USEFUL DENIAL.

The following Denial has proved of the greatest value to many: *"I DENY, to all or any, the power to Influence me against my best interests—I Am my own Master."* These words may seem simple, but if you will use them you will be surprised at their efficacy. You realize, of course, that it is the Mental State aroused by the words, that "does the work," rather than any special virtue in the words themselves.

GUARD AGAINST "IMPULSES."

2. Guard yourself from acting upon "impulses." When you feel a sudden or unaccountable "impulse" to do this thing, or that thing, stop and assert your Positive Individuality, and then drive out all outside influences, by repeating the Affirmations, etc., given above, and by creating the proper Mental Picture. Then, when you have recovered your balance, consider the impulse, and decide whether it is to your best interests, or otherwise. You will be able to see this clearly, by reason of your "mental house-cleaning" a moment before. Then, if the impulse seems to be against your best interests, drive it from you, saying: *"I drive you away from me—you do not belong to me—return to those who sent you,"* or other words to that effect. This may be rendered more forceful if you will but create a Mental Picture of the discarded idea flying away from you in the shape of a tiny thought-wave. These Mental Pictures aid one very materially in such matters, both in the sending forth of an idea, as well as in the discarding of one.

THE POSITIVE AURA.

3. Cultivate the picture and idea of a Positive

Aura, and always think of yourself as being encased in such a one. See yourself as a strong Positive "I"—a Centre of Power—encased in an Impregnable Sheath of Auric Force. You will thus be able to build up yourself into a mighty Centre. You will be surprised at the confused manner of people who try to influence you, when they come in contact with this Aura, and find their Suggestions and Mentative Currents being cast back upon themselves. Such people find themselves "all broken up" when they meet a condition like this, which they do not understand for very few of them are practical occultists. The Mental Picture of yourself as a Centre of Power, surrounded with a Positive Aura, will, if persisted in, render you extremely Positive, so that your influence is sure to be felt by the world with which you come in contact.

AMUSING SEQUELS.

You will often be amused by occurrences following after the rejection of these "stray impulses," etc. You will find that if you have had an impulse to buy a certain thing, or sell a certain thing at a sacrifice, that in a day or so, perhaps an hour or so, you will be approached by some person who will advise you personally to do that same thing, the person being likely to be benefited by the scheme or plan. I do not mean that such person has necessarily tried to influence you by Mentative Currents, for he may not have consciously done so, but nevertheless that is just what has happened, and his Desire or Will has caused these Currents to flow in your direction, and you have felt them. Now that your eyes have been opened to this fact, you will be amused and surprised to see how many corroborative proofs you will receive. But always assert your Individuality as a Centre of Power, and all will be well with you in these matters.

THE PROTECTIVE AGENT.

I hope that the above reproduction of the advice given in "Mental Magic" will do you good. And once more remember the power of the POSITIVE DENIAL as a Protective Agent. By its use you may disperse and scatter the Mentative Currents of others and surround yourself with an impregnable armor of Mentative Energy. And also remember this, which I have not said elsewhere, that the Law of Life is concerned with the Protection of the Individual, and gives to each the weapons with which to preserve his Individuality. So true is this that occultists know that there is the greatest difference in the use of the Mentative Power as an Attacking Force, and as a Protective Force. I will illustrate this briefly.

PROTECTIVE INDIVIDUALITY.

A man's Mentative Force is immensely more powerful when he uses it to Protect his Individuality than when he uses it to Attack the Individuality of another. In fact, if *everyone* understood the laws of Mentative Defence, and would avail himself of the information given by me under this head, there would be almost a total absence of Mentative Attack, for the futility of the same would soon be recognized. The only reason that the Strong Individuals are able to affect the weaker ones so frequently is because the other do not know their inner Power, and make no defense—in fact, the majority of people do not know of these laws at all; and, if one tells them, they sneer and smile knowingly, tapping their foreheads to indicate that their informant is "just a little off." Poor sheep, and geese, they are so happy in their ignorance and conceit that it almost seems a pity to disturb them.

NATURE'S PROTECTIVE POWER.

But to return to my subject. You will find that it will require a much less effort of Will to protect your Individuality than it will to attack the Individuality of another. You will find that the Law is on your side when you say, "I WON'T be influenced—I DENY the power of another to weaken my Individuality," for you have then called into operation that Law of Nature which is always in operation, and which she gives to her creatures in the way of an instinctive protective force. So there is no occasion to be afraid—

you are immune from attacks if you will but assert the Force within you.

THE GLORY OF INDIVIDUALITY.

And now, friends, in conclusion I beg of you to remember that you are Individuals—Centres of Mind, Power, Force and Energy, yes, Centres of LIFE, in the great Ocean of Being. Each of you is something different from any other Centre, and the Law wishes you to live your own life; develop your own individuality; assert your own birthright—and in the measure that you so do, so will the Law be on your side. Do not let the snare of Personal Pride trip you up, and entangle you in its meshes, for it is but an illusion. But glory in your Pride of Individuality, and do not be frightened, coaxed, seduced, lured, or driven by the Race-Thought into the condition of "the worm-of-the-dust" person—do not be a "human door-mat"—do not be a human sheep or goose, following some fool leader in a stately goose-step, or the sheep-like "follow my leader" fashion. Remember that you are Men and Women—that you are Individuals for which the cosmic machinery has been laboring for ages in order to evolve.

THE STATEMENT OF INDIVIDUALITY.

The Statement of Individuality that "I AM HERE, NOW," is a mighty one. It will always be "I Am" with you—it will always be "Here" with you—it will always be "Now" with you. No matter what state your Individuality may reach; no matter what point of space you may occupy; no matter what period of time it may be—it will always be true that "I AM, HERE, NOW!" For it will always be your "I" that is speaking—it will always be "Am" with you—everywhere place will be "Here" to you—all time will be "Now" with you. May you unfold into a perception of this Statement of Individuality. For when you do, you will have reached a mental plane where even the principles herein taught will seem elementary to you—for you will have soared above them and their operation. May this and other works of mine be as ladders upon which you may mount—and which you may then kick away from under your feet as no longer needed.

Students, I thank you—and bid you *Auf Wiedersehen!* May the Law protect you till we meet again!

FINIS.